MICHAEL MASON   BASIL GREENHILL   ROBIN CRAIG

THE BRITISH SEAFARER

HUTCHINSON/BBC
IN ASSOCIATION WITH
THE NATIONAL MARITIME MUSEUM

DISCOVERED

'The sea is natural to fishes, and the land to men'

SIR RICHARD HAWKINS

This book is derived from another medium: radio – or, as it is perhaps better described today, airborne audio. Its textual material is almost entirely drawn from the programmes of BBC Radio 4's twenty-six part serial history *The British Seafarer*, first broadcast in 1980, and its three composers are the producer and two chief advisers to the series. And this brings us to a crucial point, in the method we have used to present the seafarer rather more in his own right and rather less in the mirror of the literature of the shore. The audio series is, as far as possible, a 'vox-pop' history, composed not of written scripts but of mosaics of the seafarer's own words; the emerging picture may be debated, but it is at least made out of the recorded views of the men who actually made the history itself. In this book we have tried, as far as possible, to draw the verbal text entirely from the same sources, with the minimum of presentation by ourselves; and, as far as the visual images are concerned, to make maximum use of the actual persons, and artefacts of the seafaring story.

There are few countries to which the sea has been more important than it has been to Britain, and indeed in the common imagination of the British, ships and sailors have been endowed with a powerful mythology which ranges all the way from the Armada Medal – 'God blew with His breath and they were scattered' – through Victorian music-hall songs and sailor suits for Edwardian infants to the genius of Joseph Conrad. The British have been genuinely convinced for centuries that they are a race of island seadogs, with a special inheritance of courage, skill and love of 'the grey widow-maker'. But this legendary status of the British seafarer has in fact rather more to do with the imagination of literary landsmen than the actual experience or rewards of going to sea, and in fact maritime history remains – amazingly, given our national history – the great underprivileged subject of the British academic world. At the time of writing there is not a single university Chair of Maritime History in the whole of the British Isles. The image of seafaring which holds so popular a place in the minds of the landlubber majority is to a considerable extent yo-ho-ho-ery and romantic popularization, however loving and of however high a quality; the realities of seafaring have always been even more remarkable than these imaginations, but commonly very different. A good focusing symbol of this gulf between popular picture and fact is one of Britain's best known songs of the sea, *Heart of Oak*:

'Now cheer up, my lads, 'tis to glory we steer,
To add something more to this wonderful year:
'Tis to honour we call you, as freemen not slaves
For who are so free as the sons of the waves?'

That lyric was written by the eighteenth-century actor David Garrick in the very middle of that period when the manpower needs of Britain's navy could only be met by the mass kidnappings of the pressgang and the scouring of the jails; the sons of the waves were so reluctant to steer to glory that on the whole they could be induced to do so only by being knocked on the head and carried off bodily. John Nicol, who actually *did* volunteer during this period, said frankly that he was amazed to find he had scarcely any counterparts, and that the majority of his companions had been pressganged; Samuel Leech, who also volunteered and later wished he hadn't, attributed the defeat of his frigate by an American one in the War of 1812 partly to the superior morale of men who were serving for two years only under a discipline which, after his subsequent desertion to the United States Navy, he found much less brutal. But the printed memoirs of Nicol and Leech are rare bibliophile's items, and *Heart of Oak* has been sung by patriotic baritones from 1759 to the present day.

There is not much harm in the landsman revelling in tales of rounding the Horn or declaiming to himself

'Whither, O splendid ship, with thy white sails crowding . . .'

while toasting his toes in front of the fire and rejoicing in the fact that he is one of a race of sea kings; but the professional seaman, coping realistically with the boredoms, constraints and risks of what is still one of the most dangerous of occupations, and dreaming of a final comfortable retirement ashore, is likely to take a more hardheaded view of the economics, hardships and status of his trade. And that gulf between the actual business of 'using the sea' – the revealingly practical traditional phrase – and looking at it from a beach or through a book, is widened by the fact that the seafarer has always existed in a world which floats on its own loneliness as his ship floats on the sea and the world itself floats in space – a world very much cut off from that of the shore.

The depressed actual status with which that shore society rewarded in practice those whom it professed to admire so much in theory: the long absences, the highly artificial constraints and constrictions of life at sea, the possession of an intense common experience of which the landsman has no idea – all these things have always tended to make the seaman isolated, hard put to it to communicate the reality of his life to others and often not much concerned about trying to. And if he has tried to, he has often ended up with his tongue half in his cheek, spinning the yarns traditionally expected of him.

Ashore, he has been extensively preyed upon as long as he had money to spend, and extensively disapproved of for spending it by celebrating release

from the tensions of the voyage in drinking, brawling and womanizing. Afloat, he has been, for most of his history, vilely fed, worse housed, underpaid, over-worked and thrown on the rubbish heap to beg as soon as rupture, alcoholism, syphilis or an amputated leg meant that his strength could no longer be profitably bought, to lie out along the yardarm in the roaring darkness to gather up the leaden and icy canvas, with not so much one hand for himself and one for the ship as two hands for the ship and a pious hope that the footrope wouldn't break. If, in spite of all this, seamen have still to a surprising extent chosen the sea out of plain romantic adventurousness, and continued to be fascinated by it and its ships while cursing its hardships, exploitations and brutalities, this is their privilege, and one which the landsman should not presume upon vicariously. The realities of seafaring have been economically hardheaded and sociologically scandalous (but so were the realities of agriculture, mining, iron founding and hat making). For the most part they have been singularly un-romantic at the time, however much they may have become glamorized in later memory; and it is in this 'demythologized' state that we have tried to present them; because the reality is far more amazing than the romantic fantasies of Hollywood or the *Boys' Own Paper*. And it has to be remembered, too, that this reality is one shaped from outside by extremely utilitarian considerations.

When you have said all there is to say – and it is much – about adventurousness, the itch for achievement, exploration, warfare and all the rest, the ship is basically a piece of machinery for moving things from A to B. Seafaring, including exploration and warfare both, is basically about trade; and it is the economic and technological facts of trade – where it goes, of what kind it is, who conducts it and why – which have shaped this seafaring world, and shaped it from land. The seaman, freezing or baking in his tiny, stinking fo'c'sle, or fighting the wheel to keep his ship from broaching to in a following sea, lives in a separated world of his own which is often highly specialized – deepsea trawling, or the West Indies trade, or the P and O, or giant tankers and so on – and it is the wider framing perspective of the landsman's society which, ironically enough, explains what all this extraordinary activity is *for*. And it is, of course, an extraordinary activity. Given the alien and over-whelming nature of the oceans as an environment, it is a staggering human achievement that men should have ever 'used the sea'. In terms of skill, courage, discipline and technological ingeniousness, everyday seafaring is and has always been an enormous heroic epic – and all the more so because so much of the story is salt sores, the stench of bilges and weevilly biscuits.

The strength of the visual image is communication in totality rather than in parts, by area rather than through linear sequence; and this book is correspondingly patterned in terms of theme rather than chronology, although it does have a groundswell of movement from the sixteenth century to the present day. It concentrates particularly, too, on the archetypally typical rather than the exceptional, and the perennial basic experiences of seafaring that underlie the changing patterns of technology, organization and tradition; which is why images are often counterpointed with texts from other periods, and vice versa. And both texts and images are recapitulated and developed.

Our search has been for reality as opposed to fantasy; but we have not excluded from our pattern the beauty of the ship and the sea she sails on, for that beauty has been a part of the reality. The average sailing merchantman's fo'c'sle would likely have 'a smell you could lean on', and that is a more important fact about the history of seafaring than the glorious spectacle that ship could present in full sail; but the beauty was a reality too, and one of which seamen were strongly aware, as witness innumerable lovingly executed pictures and models. All that matters is to give these realities an appropriate order of priority. And we have to remember, too, that here again the sober utilitarian matrix is always present, shaping and forming; most of the beauty of marine technology – though not quite all – is a severely functional beauty, the aim of which is not aesthetic luxury but extremely practical purpose.

This book is dedicated, then, to the British sailor; not the Jolly Jack Tar of music-hall song or the hero or antihero of the novelist, but that comparatively unknown figure of reality, always somewhat remote, strange and lonely in relation to the majority of his fellow citizens, yet as remarkable as anything which their imaginations substituted for him.

We wish to express our indebtedness to the BBC, which created the radio broadcasts which created this book; to the National Maritime Museum and its staff, without whose generous co-operation neither broadcasts nor book could have been possible; and above all to the team of distinguished experts whose researches both produced the documentary *objets trouvés* of this history and played a vital part in working out how it should be presented. Their learning and authority have shaped our work to a degree which it would be hard to overestimate, and the riches of its material must be largely credited to them. But the editorial responsibility for the views and approach of this book is ours and ours alone, for better or for worse.

MICHAEL MASON
BASIL GREENHILL
ROBIN CRAIG

EDITORIAL CONSULTANTS

Kenneth Andrews, Reader in History, University of Hull

Ralph Davis, Professor of Economic History, University of Leicester

Alan Stimson, Curator of Navigation, National Maritime Museum, Greenwich

Peter Mathias, Chichele Professor of Economic History, All Souls College, Oxford

Piers Mackesy, Fellow of Pembroke College, Oxford

Ewan Corlett, Chairman, Burness, Corlett & Partners

Keith Matthews, Chairman, Maritime History Group, Memorial University of Newfoundland, St. John's

Michael Stammers, Keeper of Maritime History, Merseyside County Museums

Campbell MacMurray, Research Assistant, Department of Printed Books and Manuscripts, National Maritime Museum, Greenwich

Christopher Daniel, Head of Museum Services, National Maritime Museum, Greenwich

Henry Baynham, Head of History Department, Canford School

Sarah Palmer, Lecturer in History, Queen Mary College, University of London

Norman McCord, Professor of Social History, University of Newcastle upon Tyne

Peter Nailor, Professor of History, Royal Naval College, Greenwich

Alastair Couper, Professor of Maritime Studies, Institute of Science and Technology, University of Wales, Cardiff

This book is based upon the BBC Radio 4 series *The British Seafarer*

At the corner I stopped to take my last look at the crew of the *Narcissus*. They were swaying irresolute and noisy on the broad flagstones before the Mint. They were bound for the Black Horse, where men in fur caps, with brutal faces and in shirt sleeves, dispense out of varnished barrels the illusions of strength, mirth, happiness; the illusion of splendour and poetry of life, to the paid-off crews of southern-going ships. From afar I saw them discoursing, with jovial eyes and clumsy gestures, while the sea of life thundered into their ears ceaseless and unheeded. And swaying about there on the white stones, surrounded by the hurry and clamour of men, they appeared to be creatures of another kind – lost, alone, forgetful, and doomed; they were like castaways, like reckless and joyous castaways, like mad castaways making merry in the storm and upon an insecure ledge of a treacherous rock. The roar of the town resembled the roar of topping breakers, merciless and strong, with a loud voice, and cruel purpose; but overhead the clouds broke; a flood of sunshine streamed down the walls of grimy houses. The dark knot of seamen drifted in sunshine. To the left of them the trees in Tower Gardens sighed, the stones of the Tower, gleaming, seemed to stir in the play of light, as if remembering suddenly all the great joys and sorrows of the past, the fighting prototypes of these men; press gangs; mutinous cries; the wailing of women by the riverside, and the shouts of men welcoming victories.

JOSEPH CONRAD, 1895

I think I may make bold to say, that there is neither
any other mechanical or mathematical thing in the world
that is more beautiful or curious in texture than this
my watch or timekeeper for the longitude; and I heartily
thank almighty God that I have lived so long, as in some
measure to complete it.

JOHN HARRISON, 1763

1
VISIONS AND FACTS

Going to sea combines hard economic necessity with creative and imaginative courage. The movement from the sea's romantic (landbased) mythology to its realities is one from visions to economics and mechanics – and back again: seafaring life evolves continually, remorselessly, remarkably.

The art of navigation demonstrateth how, by the shortest good way, by the aptest direction, and in the shortest time, a sufficient ship, between any two places (in passage navigable) assigned, may be conducted: and in all storms and natural disturbances chancing, how to use the best possible means whereby to recover the place first assigned.

DR JOHN DEE, 1570

. . . he couldn't navigate from here to there –
he couldn't navigate a turd round a pisspot . . .

SEAMAN HERBERT GREATWOOD, 1914–18

Moving in fascination over the deep sea he could not enter, man
found ways to probe its depths, he let down nets to capture its life,
he invented mechanical eyes and ears that could re-create for his
senses a world long lost, but a world that, in the deepest part of his
And yet he has returned to his mother sea only on her own

Dar'st thou aid mutinous
    Dutch,
    and dar'st thou lay
Thee ships' wooden
    sepulchres, a prey
To leaders' rage, to storms,
    to shot, to dearth?
Dar'st thou dive seas,
    and dungeons of the
    earth?
Hast thou courageous fires
    to thaw the ice
Of frozen north
    discoveries?
            and thrice
Colder than salamanders,
    like divine
Children in the'oven,
    fires of Spain, and the
    Line,
Whose countries limbecks
    to our bodies be,
Cans't thou for gain bear?

    JOHN DONNE, 1595

ORBIS TERRÆ COMPENDIOSA DESCRIPTI

subconscious mind, he had never wholly forgotten.

terms. He cannot control or change the ocean as, in his brief tenancy of earth, he has subdued and plundered the continents. In the artificial world of his cities and towns, he often forgets the true nature of his planet and the long vistas of its history, in which the existence of the race of men has occupied a mere moment of time. The sense of all these things comes to him most clearly in the course of a long ocean voyage, when, alone in this world of water and sky, he feels the loneliness of his earth in space.

RACHEL
CARSON,
1951

The sea goes round and round, like a blood stream pumped by a mighty heart, and the heart is the heat of the sun. In North Atlantic, South Atlantic, both Pacifics and the Indian Ocean, wind, sun, and earth's rotation set up a surface water movement. No man could make long ocean voyages until first the ways of the ocean currents and winds were understood.

ALAN VILLIERS, 1963

We are now approaching lunar sunrise, and for all the people back on earth, the crew of Apollo 8 has a message that we would like to send to you. 'In the beginning God created the heaven and the earth, and the earth was without form and void and darkness was upon the face of the deep. And the spirit of God moved upon the face of the waters . . .'

APOLLO 8 ASTRONAUT, 1968

. . . And yet man has returne

The water in the depths represents the unconscious. In the depths as a rule is a treasure guarded by a serpent or dragon. In order to recover the treasure the dragon has to be overcome.

C. G. JUNG, 1936

his mother sea only on her own terms . . .

The shark or Tiberune, is a fish
like unto those which we call
dogfishes, but that he is far greater
. . . he is much hated of seafaring
men . . . It is the most ravenous
fish known in the sea; for he
swalloweth all that he findeth. In
the pouch of them hath been found
hats, caps, shoes, shirts, legs and
arms of men, ends of ropes, and
many other things . . .

SIR RICHARD HAWKINS, 1603

All put in order, I luffed near the shore, to give my farewell to all the inhabitants of the town of Plymouth, whereof the most part were gathered on the Hoe, to show their grateful correspondency to the love and zeal which I, my father, and predecessors have ever borne to that place, as to our natural and mother town. And first with my noise of trumpets, after with my waits, and then with my other music, and lastly with the artillery of my ships, I made the best signification I could, of a kind farewell. This they answered with the waits of the town, and the ordinance on the shore, and with shouting of voices, which with the fair evening and silence of the night, were heard a great distance off.

SIR RICHARD HAWKINS, 1603

Whenever I land (if I ever do), I shall come to a country of strangers, unknowing and unknown to all but my own family.

ADMIRAL COLLINGWOOD, 1809

For, which of the kings of this land before Her Majesty had their banners ever seen in the Caspian Sea? . . . What English ships did heretofore ever anchor in the mighty River of Plate? pass and re-pass the unpassable (in former opinion) Strait of Magellan, range along the coast of Chile, Peru, and all the backside of Nova Hispania, further than any Christian ever passed, traverse the mighty breadth of the South Sea . . . enter into alliance, amity and traffic with the princes of the Moluccas, and the Isle of Java, double the famous Cape of Bona Speranza, arrive at the Isle of Santa Helena, and last of all return home most richly laden with the commodities of China, as the subjects of this now flourishing monarchy have done?

RICHARD HAKLUYT, 1589

Our way, to my great delight, lay along the quay and beside the great multitude of ships of all sizes and rigs and nations. In one, sailors were singing at their work; in another, there were men aloft, high over my head, hanging to threads that seemed no thicker than a spider's . . . I saw the most wonderful figureheads, that had all been far over the ocean. I saw, besides, many old sailors, with rings in their ears, and whiskers curled in ringlets, and tarry pigtails, and their swaggering, clumsy, sea-walk; and if I had seen as many kings or archbishops I could not have been more delighted.

ROBERT LOUIS STEVENSON, 1881

The sea is the container of the unknown and the mysterious. It is an appropriate synonym for the unconscious. The sea is the symbol of the collective unconscious, because unfathomed depths lie concealed beneath its surface.

C. G. JUNG, 1944

25-mile wide Bahama sand shoal, seen from skylab

There are fifteen times more water in the sea than the entire volume of all the exposed land. Sea covers seventy per cent of the globe – 139 million square miles of it. The sea at its deepest – in the Marianas Trench of the Pacific Ocean – is more than a mile deeper than the highest mountain.

ALAN VILLIERS, 1963

Man himself was cradled in the sea. He emerged a protoplasm, returned a fisherman and a mariner. To this day his body is three-parts water . . .

The sea gives life and takes life with an endless and tremendous abandon un-equalled – indeed, unimagin-able – anywhere on land. The surface waters of the sea, seen from below by a rising diver, abound with minute microscopic life which flits like sunbeams, too small to be seen except when the sunlight chances to fall on them. The blue whale, the largest animal ever known – it can exceed 100 feet in length, weigh over 100 tons – lives and flourishes in the ocean, so long as it can avoid man's harpoon-guns.

ALAN VILLIERS, 1963

Microscopic marine organism, seen underwater

Too proud, too proud, what a press she bore!
Royal, and all her royals wore.
Sharp with her, shorten sail!
Too late; lost; gone with the gale.

This was that fell capsize
As half she had righted and hoped to rise
Death teeming in by her portholes
Raced down decks, round messes of mortals.

Then a lurch forward, frigate and men;
'All hands for themselves' the cry ran then;
But she who had housed them thither
Was around them, bound them or wound them with her.

GERARD MANLEY HOPKINS, 1878

Sail's a lady, steam's a bundle of iron.
CAPTAIN BROMLEY, 1964

They say who saw one corpse cold
He was all of lovely manly mould
Every inch a tar
Of the best we boast our sailors are.

Look, foot to forelock, how all things suit! He
Is strung by duty, is strained to beauty
And brown-as-dawning-skinned
With brine and shine and whirling wind.

GERARD MANLEY HOPKINS, 1878

Especially in foul weather, the labour, hazard, wet and cold is so incredible I cannot express it . . . they are so over-charged with labour, bruises and overstraining themselves (for there is no dallying nor excuses with storms, gusts, overgrown seas, and lee shores). Men of all other professions, in lightning, thunder, storms and tempests, with rain and snow, may shelter themselves in dry houses, by good fires, and good cheer; but those are the chief times, that seamen must stand to their tacklings, and attend with all diligence their greatest labour upon the decks.

CAPTAIN JOHN SMITH, 1627

For it is not enough to be a seaman, but it is necessary to be a painstaking seaman . . . for I do not allow any to be a good seaman that hath not undergone the most offices about a ship, and that hath not in his youth been both taught and inured to all labours; for to keep a warm cabin and lie in sheets is the most ignoble part of a seaman; but to endure and suffer, as, a hard cabin, cold and salt meat, broken sleeps, mouldy bread, dead beer, wet clothes, want of a fire – all these are aboard, besides boat, lead, topyards, anchor-moorings and the like.

LUKE FOX, 1631

I am Gideon Sanders of Brading in the Isle of Wight, formerly of London, aged thirty-four: I have been at sea since I was eight or ten years of age, and have made a hundred voyages in my time both in trade of merchandise and of warfare; wherof I have made ten or twelve voyages with letters of reprisal, first with Captain Fenton in the *Galleon Leicester*, and afterwards four voyages with Captain Riman in the *Lion* and the *Swiftsure*, and the *Disdain*; since, I served in a carvel of one Pittes of Bristol, and the *Diamond* of Bridgewater . . .

GIDEON SANDERS, 1591

It is a serious relation, that in which a man
stands to his ship. A ship is a creature
which we have brought into the world, as
it were on purpose to keep us up to the
mark. In her handling a ship will not put
up with a mere pretender.

JOSEPH CONRAD, 1906

. . . The *Merchant Royal*
The *Endeavour*
The *Four Friends*
The *Bark Buggins*
The *Belle of the Niger*
The *Waterwitch*
The *Maid of Athens*
The *Lindisfarne*
The *Ocean Bride*
The *Elizabeth Drew*
The *Fortune*
The *Sovereign of the Seas*
The *Sultan*
The *James and Mary*
The *Tillie E. Starbuck*
The *Victory*
The *Mary Miller*
The *Diolinda* . . .

As far as we were concerned it was just
a routine . . . You can look back on it, you know . . .
on your younger life and on this deep-sea carry-on, there
was a tremendous lot of romance in it. You saw all kinds
of things you wouldn't have had the chance of seeing
if you'd worked ashore. There's a lot besides that
you lose in life, but you gain a lot in life . . .
Seafaring people, after they have been to
sea all the years of their life, there's
something they've lost in themselves, eh?
They keep theirselves to theirselves
and their family, they are not
interested in anybody else,
perhaps, and it is something within
them that they have lost that the people
ashore doesn't lose. I think that takes
effect when you are quite young, you get this
aloofness . . . As you get older it digs more
deeper into you . . .

ANTHONY MORDUE, 1971

I am Nicholas Bailye of Bristol, trumpeter, aged 28 years or thereabouts: I know the *Minion* of Bristol, which is of the burthen of nine score tons or thereabouts, and therein served this last voyage these persons following:

Thomas Webb, *Captain*

George Whittington of Bristol,
   lieutenant

Humphrey Withers of Hampton,
   Master

Richard Hughes

John Elderton of Hampton

William Browne of Bristol

John Lane of Minehead

Michael Calverley, of the same place,
   master's mates

Peter Edwards of Hampton,
   gunner

Henry Peach

John Spragge,
   gunner's mates

Thomas Proute of Bristol,
   boatswain . . .

with others, whose names I remember not . . .

NICHOLAS BAILYE, 1596

Bideford, November 27th 1684

Mr Nicholas Bear: We desire you to take the first opportunity of a fair wind and tide that God shall vouchsafe and sail out over the Bar with our ship *Vineyard*, and if possible, to stop in the Road of Clovelly so long as to take in twenty-three barrels of herrings from Mr Benjamin Croker, from thence directly for Waterford in the Kingdom of Ireland, there to address yourself to Mr Richard Mabanke, Merchant, whom we desire to provide for you such provisions as amount to one hundred pounds or thereabouts, the particulars of which goes with you to him unsealed. You are to take care that it be all very good. If freight present to the place you are bound, you may embrace it and when you have gotten all on board, which we hope you will do with all expedition, that then you sail directly for Mountserrat in the West Indies, there to dispose of all such goods, wares and merchandises as you carry along with you on our account to the best advantage. If you have any room to spare you may take in some freight if it offers, for this place, and when your business is over to come directly home to Bideford. We hope that your care, prudence and diligence will be such (in the management of all our affairs) that may make much for your credit and honour, and have the continuance of the favour and respects of

   Your loving friends John Darracott, Edward Wren, Robert Wren

(Mr Bear, if you are disappointed in anything above said, that then you may have the liberty to do with our ship and goods as you think for our best advantage.)

MERCHANT SEAMEN'S ACT—7 & 8 VICT., CAP. 112.

SCHEDULE E.

CERTIFICATE OF DISCHARGE.

This is to Certify, That _____ served as _____ of the Port of _____ day of _____ 18__

whose Register Ticket is numbered _____ and that he was discharged from the said Ship

on board the "_____" of the Burthen of _____ Tons, from the _____ day of _____ 18__ at _____ N.B.

Dated this _____ day of _____ Master.

Certificate _____ given to every Person comprising the Crew at the time of discharge, or of _____ is a Certificate of Service and Capacity merely, and has no reference to _____ of Character is an optional _____ arate affair.

CONTRACT TICKET.

... (GRAVESEND,) for MELBOURNE

_____ day of _____ 186

_____ Tons Register, to Sail from

LONDON for the Port of MELBOURNE

in PORT PHILLIP

	No. of Persons.	
	Adults above 12 Years.	Children 12 Years and under.
	1	1
	1	1

In consideration of the Sum of

150

we hereby agree with the Person named in the Margin hereof that such Person shall be provided with First-Class Cabin Passage (exclusive of Wines, Beer, and Spirits), in the above-named Ship, to sail from the Port of LONDON for the Port of MELBOURNE in PORT PHILLIP, with not less than Forty Cubical Feet of Luggage for each Person, and that such Person shall be victualled as First-Class Cabin Passenger during the Voyage and the Time of Detention at any Place before its Termination; and we further engage to land the Person aforesaid, with their Luggage, at the above-mentioned Port, free of any Charge beyond the Passage Money aforesaid; and we hereby acknowledge to have received the Sum of **150** in full payment of such Passage Money.

For MONEY WIGRAM & SONS,
7, Leadenhall Street.

_____ Morgan

_____ Charles Morgan

to be paid at 7, Leadenhall Street, Three Days before Embarkation.

LYING IN THE EAST INDIA DOCKS.

£ **150.** _____ 186

NOTICE TO CABIN PASSENGERS.

N.B. This Contract Ticket is exempt from Stamp Duty.

The old-fashioned sailor, the veritable man-before-the-mast, the sailor from boyhood up, he, tho' indeed of the same species as a landsman, is in some respects singularly distinct from him. The sailor is frankness, the landsman is finesse. Life is not a game with the sailor, demanding the long head; no intricate game of chess where few moves are made in straightforwardness, and ends are attained by indirection

HERMAN MELVILLE, 1891

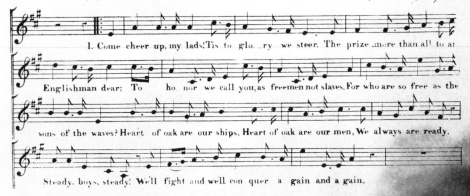

Heart of Oak?

Words by David Garrick, 1759.   Music by Dr. Boyce 1759.

1. Come cheer up, my lads! Tis to glo ry we steer. The prize more than all to an Englishman dear; To ho nor we call you, as freemen not slaves, For who are so free as the sons of the waves? Heart of oak are our ships, Heart of oak are our men, We always are ready, Steady, boys, steady! We'll fight and well con quer a gain and a gain.

We had only been in action a few minutes when the Admiral's Secretary came across to where the Torpedo Officer was stationed in the conning tower and drew attention to the *Indefatigable*. He crossed at once to the starboard side and laid his glasses on her. While he was still looking at her through his glasses, she was hit by two shells, one on the foc'sle and one on the fore turret. Both shells appeared to explode on impact. Then there was an interval of about thirty seconds, during which there was absolutely no sign of fire, or flame, or smoke, except the little actually formed by the burst of the two shells, which was not considerable. At the end of this interval, the ship completely blew up, commencing apparently from for'ard. The main explosion started with sheets of flame, followed immediately afterwards by a dense, dark smoke, which obscured the ship from view. All sorts of stuff was blown high in the air, a 60-foot steam picket boat, for example, being blown about 200 feet, apparently intact, though upside down.

NAVIGATING OFFICER, HMS *New Zealand*, 1916

People may talk of negro slavery and the whip, but let them look nearer home, and see a poor sailor arrived from a long voyage, exulting in the pleasure of soon being among his dearest friends and relations. Behold him just entering the door, when a pressgang seizes him like a felon, drags him away and puts him into the tender's hold, and from thence he is sent on board a man-of-war, perhaps ready to sail to some foreign station, without seeing either his wife, friends or relations; if he complains he is likely to be seized up and flogged with a cat, much more severe than the negro driver's whip, and if he deserts he is flogged round the fleet, nearly to death

WILLIAM RICHARDSON, c. 1810

HONI SOIT QVI MALY PENSE

Ie Maine   Tiendray

Great Britains
Coasting Pylot
BEING
A NEW SURVEY
OF THE
Sea Coast
By Capt.
GREENVILE COLLINS
HYDROGRAPHER
to their
MAJESTYS
1693

. . . and yet man has returned to his mother sea
only on her own terms . . .

I am informed by the Chairman of the Health and Safety
Commission that the fatal accident incidence rate among divers
working around offshore installations and on pipelines in the
United Kingdom sector of the North Sea was 6 per 1,000 in 1975
and 7 per 1,000 in 1976. A comparable figure for 1977 is not yet
available.

Direct comparisons with other occupations may be misleading
because of the intermittent character of diving work. However, fatal
accident incidence rates per 1,000 at risk in other industries are as
follows:

Deep sea trawling	3.160
Construction	0.181
Shipbuilding	0.140
All manufacturing industry	0.037
Mining	0.247

JOHN GRANT, *Secretary of State for Employment*, 1978

It shouldn't happen, but things happen so quickly that . . . you
know, when you've got weather and tide against you, what do you
do? I mean, where minutes are of vital importance and you can't get
a standby diver in the water quick enough, and there's nothing very
much you can do . . .

MASTER, OIL RIG *Sea Quest*, 1977

I saw that if
I went to sea when
I should be grown
in years I should be
little better than a
slave, going with many a
hungry belly and wet
back, and being always called
'old dog' and 'old rogue' and
'son of a whore'. But all people
are not born to live at ease. My
desire was from my youth to see
strange countries and fashions and
I must with hunger and cold pay for it.

EDWARD BARLOW, 1668

THE SEPARATE WORLD

The ship sails in the sea like the
earth in space and is itself a
concrete symbol of the isolated
closed and highly specialized
world of the seafarer: hardship
grindingly hard work, sudden
stresses, monotony, skill
balanced like a gyroscope
on the sailing ship's
pivotal ability to
tack against the
wind

In those vast
solitudes in the
Pacific the feeling is
often overwhelming to any
thinking man. I have been for
four months without seeing even a
sail. Nothing but the fish and the
waters, and often very few of the fish
The common seamen are often very
oppressed by the long, long solitudes
SHIP'S CARPENTER, 1850

Ours was a ship of the best sort as regards its management and accommodation – no false weights and no humbug about fines or such like, to cheat the men and please the owners; but there's a great deal of it about. The owners in the African trade are good men generally. It's your cheap owners mostly in other trades that pluck every feather out of a seaman if they can, and they always can somehow.

SEAMAN, 1850

Many seamen are of that lazy, idle temper, that let them alone and they never care for doing anything that they should do, and when they do anything it is with a grumbling unwilling mind, so that they must be forced and drove to it, which is a great trouble and vexation to those men that overlook them, and many times are forced to strike them against their will when fair means will not do it.

EDWARD BARLOW, 1694

AGREEMENT AND ACCOUNT
(FOREIGN-GOING SHIP.)

It was my lot to fall into the hands of Jack Gillies, than whom a handier fellow never left the Emerald Isle.

'Let us have the necessaries first, Robert,' said he, 'and we will attend to other matters afterwards.' Jack had been at sea ever since he was the height of a marlinspike, and a better practical sailor was not to be found from stem to stern. From the knotting of a rope yarn to the steering of a ship under bare poles in a typhoon, Jack excelled in all. No one could surpass him at the manoeuvring of a thirty-two pounder; he was an excellent sailmaker too, and there was not a sail aboard, from the windsail to the spanker, but what he could shape and make.

LANDSMAN HAY, c. 1805

All the lads aboard the ships, the steamships y'know, 'ad leather seaboots. But they was no good aboard of a sailing ship. Well, you're climbing up the rigging aboard of a sailing ship. All you wanted aboard of a sailing ship was a good, old, thick, heavy cloth overcoat. But no oilskins . . . these'd get blown over your head y'know . . . same as heavy seaboots, they were no good. I used to hear the lads, 'Oh', he says, 'you don't want a good pair o' them, like, to go up aloft a ship. All you want is an old ragged pair of boots,' he said, 'wi' a good pair of heels' – for the footropes you know. Seaboots an' oilskins was no good up aloft.

JOHN ROBERTSON, 1971

In stormy weather, when the ship rolled and tumbled, as though some great millstone were rolling up one hill and down another, being gotten up into the tops, there we must hale and pull to make fast the sail, seeing nothing but the air above us and the water beneath us, and that so raging as though every wave would make a grave for us: and many times in nights so dark that we could not see one another, and blowing so hard that we could not hear one another speak.

EDWARD BARLOW, 1661

The sailors are the ancient men for hoysing the sails, getting the tacks aboard, hauling the bowlines, and steering the ship.

The younkers are the young men called foremastmen to take in the topsails, or top-and-yard; furl and sling the mainsail; bowsing or tricing; and take their turn at helm.

CAPTAIN JOHN SMITH, 1627

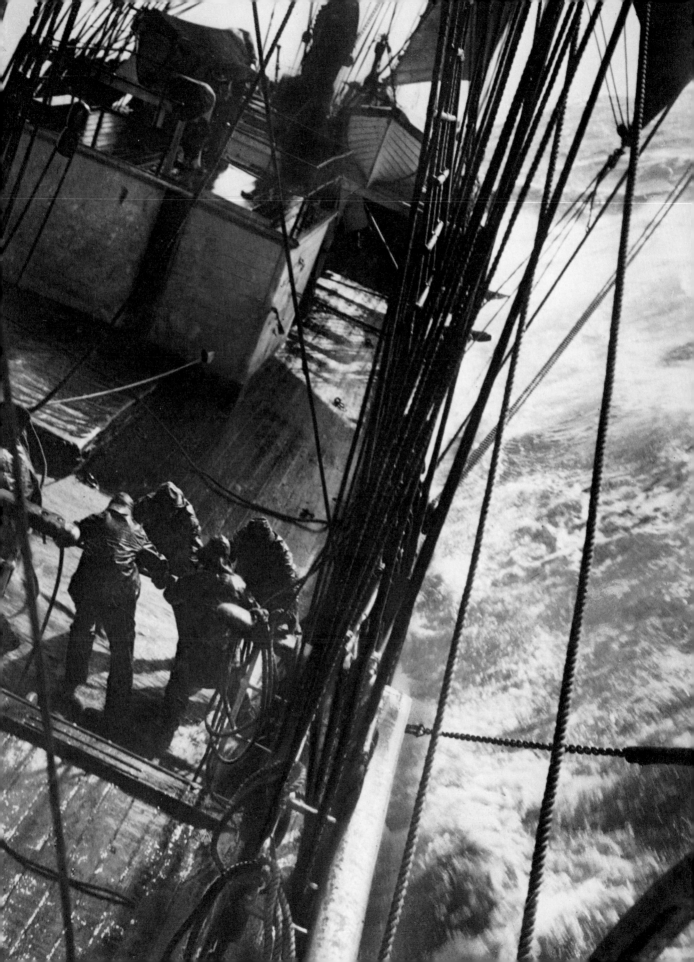

We pumped all night, all day, all the week – watch and watch. She was working herself loose, and leaked badly – not enough to drown us at once, but enough to kill us with the work at the pumps. And while we pumped the ship was going from us piecemeal: the bulwarks went, the stanchions were torn out, the ventilators smashed, the cabin door burst in. There was not a dry spot in the ship. She was being gutted bit by bit. And we pumped. And there was no break in the weather. The sea was white like a sheet of foam, like a caldron of boiling milk; there was not a break in the clouds, no – not the size of a man's hand – no, not for so much as ten seconds. There was for us no sky, there were for us no stars, no sun, no universe – nothing but angry clouds and an infuriated sea. We pumped watch and watch, for dear life; and it seemed to last for months, for years, for all eternity.

JOSEPH CONRAD, 1902

All of a sudden I happened to look out on the port quarter. I saw a great wall . . . a black wall of water with a white curl of foam running along the top, and I looked at it and I thought to myself, that is not a wave, that is a tidal wave. So I dropped me mitts – I was putting my mitts on – and rushed up the fo'c'sle ladder and grabbed the rail and I yelled out to the man on the lookout, I said, grab the rail, I said, that will smash us. And it struck us and it went off like a dozen guns, lifted her stern up, drove her head down and she came up again and lifted up enough water to nearly sweep us away from where we was hanging on to this rail. I looked down on the deck and couldn't see it, all under water.

CHARLES ANDREWS, 1951

We found the anchor had started and continued to drag. The weather being very severe with an intense frost the pilot did not like to leave the cabin fire, and the captain could not get two men on deck which were benumbed with the cold. These two, with the man to helm, and the captain (four in all) made the whole crew. It was now found necessary to drop the other anchor, which was executed by myself and the captain, and we veered away the cable 'till both anchors brought her up. At daylight the brig was covered with ice and the cables very thick, the tide of flood also coming on it was determined to endeavour to get the anchors. Having secured the anchors and in attempting to work to windward the fore stay-sail blew away from the bolt rope, and the fore top-sail split on the leech, which obliged us to run for Minehead. On getting near the place we made a signal for a boat, but no one appearing we proceeded for Ilfracombe once more, our captain's finger having been frost bitten in the morning was turned very black. We got into the harbour before dark, having only about one meal of biscuits remaining on board.

SAMUEL KELLY, 1786

I remember one time, we were rollin' very heavy, in a sailin' ship, an' the bosun said, 'Go up aloft', he said 'and put a few ratlines on that topmast riggin'. It took you all your time to work with one hand, one hand for the ship, one for yourself. An' the Old Man come on deck . . . look up . . . 'Good God,' he said, 'what's that man doin' up there?' The bosun said, 'Oh', he said 'I gave him a job', he said, 'there's nothin' wrong wi' it', he said . . . 'Fetch 'im down here! Go up yourself if you see somethin' you want doin', not a young fellow like that!' Old Man! . . . and the sails . . . *shwp* . . . slappin', y'know. Yes. Life . . . hard.

JOHN ROBERTSON, 1971

It will now be well to show how the sails act upon a ship, with reference to her centre of rotation. Suppose a vessel to be rigged with three sails, one in the forward part, one at the centre, and the third at the after part, and her left or larboard side to be presented to the wind, which we will suppose to be abeam, or at right angles with the keel. If the head-sail only were set, the effect would be that the wind would send the vessel a little ahead and off to the starboard on her centre of rotation, so as to bring her stern slowly round to the wind. If the after-sail only were set, the vessel would shoot ahead a little, her stern would go off to the starboard and her head come up into the wind. If only the centre sail were set, the effect would be the same as if all three of the sails were set, and she would go ahead in a straight line.

These principles of the wind acting upon the sails, and the water upon the rudder, are the foundation of the whole science of working a ship.

R. H. DANA, 1855

Yes, your ship wants to be humoured with knowledge. You must treat with an understanding consideration the mysteries of her feminine nature, and then she will stand by you faithfully in the unceasing struggle with forces wherein defeat is no shame. A ship is not a slave. You must make her easy in a seaway, you must never forget that you owe her the fullest share of your thought, of your skill, of your self-love. If you remember that obligation, naturally and without effort, as if it were an instinctive feeling of your inner life, she will sail, stay, run for you as long as she is able, or, like a sea-bird going to rest upon the angry waves, she will lay out the heaviest gale that ever made you doubt living long enough to see another sunrise.

JOSEPH CONRAD, 1906

No man is entitled to the rate or wages of an able seaman who is not a good helmsman. If, upon fair trial, in bad weather, a seaman is found incapable of steering the ship, under circumstances not extraordinary, he would be considered by all on board to have failed of his duty.

R. H. DANA, 1855

When the wind may be going four times as fast as the ship, and the waves twice as fast, it is not to be wondered at, that ships are sometimes broached to, against the power of the helm, when sailing before the wind. None but the best helmsman should be admitted to steer at such times. A great risk attends relieving the helmsman, especially in the night; as he that is to take the helm, often comes but half awake from sleep, and takes the helm without examining where it lies at the time, and how far the ship requires it each way to confine her to the course;

thus, not considering the danger, he at first lets the ship get such a sheer, that his best endeavours cannot stop her from being broached to, or brought by the lee. To prevent which, the helmsman that is to be relieved, if he has steered well, should not quit the helm before he has shewed and made known to him that is to relieve, the particulars of her trim, and how she may be best steered at that time, how many turns and spokes of the wheel she requires to starboard and port, or to windward and leeward, to confine her to her course.

WILLIAM HUTCHINSON, *c.* 1750

'What's the mate like? what's the cook like?'

'I'll go with Captain —————; he's a taut one, but he is Captain of his own ship.'

ANONYMOUS SEAMAN, RN, *c.* 1800

The crew as far as they are known to be good and bad, should be equally divided and they should be told by the commander that the safety, ease and success of the whole depends chiefly on everyone doing or getting the necessary duty done, with watchfulness, care and diligence, according to their different stations. The watch upon deck have upon them the important charge, not only of the safety of the ship and their own lives, but the lives of the other watch and all that are below, therefore any neglect of duty by the watch upon deck, and especially in keeping a good look-out, should be resented by all the rest of the crew: the watch below should lie down with such clothes on, as to be ready to turn out directly, when all hands are called, which may be to save the whole from immediate destruction.

WILLIAM HUTCHINSON,
c. 1750

The crews are not rated by the officers after they get to sea, but, both in the merchant service and in the navy, each man rates himself when he ships. A man puts his name down and contracts for the wages and duty of a seaman, ordinary seaman, or boy, at his pleasure. Notwithstanding this license, there are very few instances of it being abused; for every man knows that if he is found incompetent to perform the duty he contracts for, his wages cannot only be reduced to the grade for which he is fitted, but that something additional will be deducted for the deception practised upon all concerned. More than this, the rest of the crew consider it a fraud upon themselves; as they are thus deprived of a man of the class the vessel required; which makes her shorthanded for the voyage, and increases the duty put upon themselves.

R. H. DANA, 1855

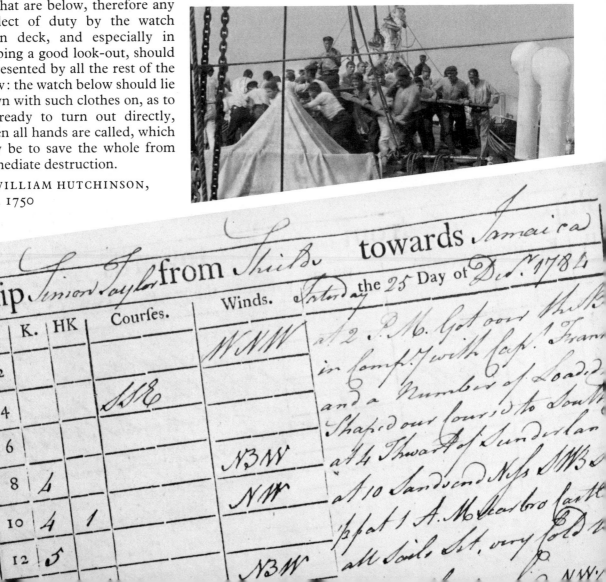

At all times the forecastle was a foulsome and suffocating abode, and in bad weather the water and filth which washed about the deck and among the chests and casks created the most intolerable and loathsome stench . . . here, however, these 14 sailors and apprentices slept, washed, dressed and had their food . . . consisting almost entirely of inferior salted pork, unpalatable beef and brown biscuits, too often mouldy and full of maggots . . . the forecastle was full of rats which found their way into the hammocks in which the crew slept. In the West Indies the place was suffocatingly hot, and in winter, when approaching the English Channel, it was as bitterly cold, no stoves or fires of any kind being allowed inward. No Siberian slaves suffered as much from the intensity of the cold as did those sailors and apprentices, their damp clothes as they lay upon the chests or hung suspended from the beams being frequently frozen to such an extent that the ice had to be beaten from them before they could be used again.

W. S. LINDSAY, c. 1890

Whereas, William White, Boatswain's mate of His Majesty's Ship *Gibraltar*, but serving on board His Majesty's Ship *Courageux*, hath been tried by a Court-Martial on charges exhibited against him by Lieutenant John Glover, for having seized him by the collar, and wishing he had the said Lieutenant Glover on shore, he would then do his business, and other mutinous expressions; and the Court having found him guilty of the twenty-second Article of the Articles of War, hath adjudged the said William White to suffer death by being hanged by the neck at the yard-arm of such Ship, as the Commanding officer for the time being might direct.

You are hereby required and directed to see the said sentence of death carried into execution upon the body of the said William White.

HORATIO NELSON, 1799

It may not be amiss to observe the private employment of the crew, and it may be easily conjectured that where two or three hundred men are assembled, that you'll find several mechanics. Here in one place may be seen a tailor, in another a shoemaker, a tinker, a brazier, a glazier, a plumber, a painter, button makers, knife makers, book binders, coopers; nay, every trade almost that you can mention, even to a watch maker, and all at their different occupations. Every sailor knows a little about his needle and can cut clothes, particularly trousers. Those who are not employed sewing or mending, you'll see them either learning to read or write, or cyphering, or instructing others. Some are playing the violin, flute, or fife, while others dance or sing thereto. Others are relating awful stories of what happened in awful times, while their hearers are listening with respectful silence.

ROBERT WILSON, c. 1800

Sailors contrive to keep up their spirits amid constant causes of depression and misery. One is a good singer, another can spin tough forecastle yarns, while a third can crack a joke with sufficient point to call out roars of laughter. But for these interludes life in a man-of-war with severe officers would be intolerable; mutiny or desertion would mark the voyages of every such ship. A casual visitor in a man-of-war, beholding the songs, the dance, the revelry of the crew, might judge them to be happy. But I know these things are often resorted to because they feel miserable, just to drive away dull care.

SAMUEL LEECH, c. 1812

Peter Owen told Captain Skevington that as long as he went fizzling to the General with tales to pick him a thank, so long they should never be in quiet. Hereon was demanded, what was a fizzler, and why privy talebearers were called fizzlers. To this was answered, that as he which fizzleth doth stink worse than a plain farter and doth also lead many into suspicion because it is not known whence the stench cometh, so – etc.

RICHARD MADOX, 1582

Captain Moody, Cutty Sark

We agreed very bad, the captain and us. When we left the Downs, we had very bad weather in the Channel, and two men were laid up sick, and sometimes three. The captain, because he couldn't get the ship worked to his liking, kept calling all hands a 'parcel of d---d soldiers'. She worked very hard with too few hands, such as the complement we had, and dreadful hard when three were laid up. The captain swore terribly. He didn't read prayers – swearing captains do, though, oft enough – by way of a set-off, they say. Nobody can respect prayers from such people. I do from good men. I am a Scotchman. My last captain was a good seaman, though not much of a navigator. He pretty well ran the ship ashore in coming into the English Channel off the Scilly Islands.

SEAMAN, 1850

Men with sailor instincts, even when asleep, were so sensitive to the motions of their vessels that the least change or jerky movement would awaken them. Small boats, such as fishing cobles, ship's pinnaces, or lifeboats, have a distinct language of their own, different from large or small sailing-vessels. This language always tells those in charge in boisterous weather whether they are handling their vessel properly or not, and if the expert who knows the mystery of boat or ship language disregards what is plainly asked of him, some trouble is sure to follow.

WALTER RUNCIMAN, c. 1890

We had a good captain, but a strict man in regard
of duty. He had worked his way 'from the hawse-pipes aft',
and knew every branch. He was a seaman, every inch of him.
But I have met with many an officer not fit to be trusted
with either life or property at sea.

SEAMAN, 1850

Each task has its man, and each man his place.
A ship contains a set of *human* machinery in which every
man is a wheel, a band or a crank, all moving with wonderful
regularity and precision to the *will* of its machinist –
the all-powerful Captain.

SAMUEL LEECH, *c.* 1812

WOOD, CANVAS, HEMP AND CLOCKS

**The threemasted wooden sailing ship –
Europe's first 'space capsule' – is a machine for
moving things from A to B. Its technology is that of agriculture
and handwork – wood, cloth, fibre, the smithy; also that
of the sophisticated shore support culture – mathematics,
astronomy, horology, cartography . . .**

A Sea Grammar,
WITH
THE PLAINE EXPOSITION
of SMITHS Accidence for young
Sea-men, enlarged.

Diuided into fifteene Chapters: what they are you
may partly conceiue by the Contents.

Written by Captaine IOHN SMITH, fometimes
Gouernour of VIRGINIA, and Admirall of
NEVV-ENGLAND.

The first and lowest timber in a ship is the keel, to which is fastened all the rest; this is a great tree or more, hewn to the proportion of her burden, laid by a right line in the bottom of the dock or stocks. At the one end is scarfed into it the stem, which is a great timber wrought compassing, and all the butt-ends of the planks forwards are fixed to it. The stern post is another great timber, which is let into the keel at the other end somewhat sloping, and from it doth rise the two fashion pieces, like a pair of great horns; to those are fastened all the planks that reach to the after end of the ship.

CAPTAIN JOHN SMITH, 1627

After our coming to Newcastle and that we lodged ourselves conveniently, we first viewed the places from whence we were to make choice of our frame and other provisions, which were Chopwell Woods and Brancepeth Park. Then, having marked such trees as were fittest our purpose, our workmen were disposed of to their several charges, and began to fell, square, and saw with all the expedition we could. God so blessed us in our proceedings that in a short time as much of the frame was made ready as laded away a great collier belonging to Woodbridge, which was safely landed at Woolwich. The 21st day of December, the keel of the great new ship was laid in his place in the dock.

PHINEAS PETT, 1635

Planking a ship is like the skin, sinews and ligaments to an animal.

Working clinch, boatbuilders use few moulds or patterns
beyond one midship section, to verify the required width
of each plank, and the equal curve of the sides as the boat
unfolds herself, plank after plank, from the keel, trusting
for the general contour and model of the boat to a
practised eye, and the bend of clean grained wood.

ROBERT C. LESLIE, 1892

Barges were built with no plans; the owner would decide
on the length, breadth, and depth, and then it was left to
the individual builder, more or less, to the shape, and
each builder had his own plans or ideas of building a
barge. Anyone in the barge trade could tell, a barge was
built in Ipswich or a barge was built in Harwich. Well,
the backbone of a barge is its keelson, which is usually
pitch pine or Oregon pine, somewhere about seventy feet
long, and from there the barge is built. Frames are put
up, floors are shaped and as the barge is being built, so
the owner would come in and discuss with the builder
whether he liked the shape or not. Very often he'd have a
piece of chalk and a piece of wood and would chalk out
the shape he thought it ought to be.

ROY ORVIS, 1966

When you build clinker, the ship takes shape under your very hands; if it doesn't turn out so well, you can finish it as you want it. Once you get over the bilge the thing is practically done.

SHIPWRIGHT, 1950

The old shipwright with his black wooden toolbox slung over his shoulder, or plying his adze or the caulking iron, is a type of a British artisan unhappily now becoming extinct. He was no ordinary workman following day after day the same monotonous job, for his work called for the constant exercise of his own individuality, of his powers of observation, and his ingenuity in the application of the teachings of experience; the selection of suitable timber, of proper scantling, oak crooks for the floors, aprons and knees, the curved timber for the futtocks, all called for skill and knowledge, and he had to keep constantly in view, when building, the necessity for giving proper shifts to the scarfs and the butting of the planks – all demanding not only thought, but daily presenting new problems which only a trained eye and experience could solve.

SIR WILLIAM FORWOOD, 1920

The Captains, Masters, Owners, and Navigators of Ships, they move in another Orb, but still act in the same Round of Business; the Ship is built, and fitted out for a Voyage; Thousands of Tradesmen and Workmen subsist upon the petty Demands of the Captain or other Persons who direct the Voyage; the Plank, the Iron-Work, the Masts, the Rigging, the Tar and Hemp, the Flax and Oil, all pass through different and numberless Hands, till they centre in the Builder's Yard; there the Frame of a Vessel is set on the Stocks. What Hands are then employed to create the beautiful useful Form of a Ship! And what Art to perfect and launch her into the Water!

The Carpenters, Caulkers, Mast-makers, Joiners, Carvers, Painters, Smiths, etc., finish the Hull; the Tradesmen are employed to furnish and fit her out; the Sail-Makers, the Rope-Makers, Anchor-Smiths, Block-Makers, Gun-Founders, Coopers, and (for a Thousand small Things too trifling to mention, though absolutely needful) the Ship Chandler, and at last the Brewer, Butcher, Baker, etc. for Provision to victual her; all help on the Voyage.

All these, supported by that glorious Head of Commerce, called the Merchant, are employed in the Outset of the Ship.

DANIEL DEFOE, 1728

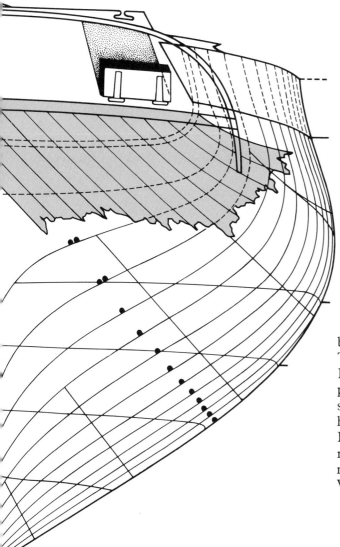

Their bottoms form the same elliptical curve or sheer downwards, as the sheer of the bends, upper works, and decks do upwards, which gives pleasure to all people of true taste for ships, that makes them say they swim in water like ducks.

WILLIAM HUTCHINSON, *c.* 1750

There are so many things proper to be known, in order to work a Ship's body, as first to draw the Draught, then to transcribe that Draught to Foot Measure (which is called laying down a Body in the Mould-loft) and afterwards to cross the Moulds, and take every Dimension proper to mould the Timber, both with Frugality in the Conversion of the Timber, and Accuracy in the Performance, that I cannot but wonder it has not been more publicly looked into. Let any one but take a serious View of the Shape of a Ship under Water, how every Timber turns itself in a different Form, and what a Complication of Matter is requisite in composing such a Machine, and he must needs admire how such a confused Piece of Work could be brought to Perfection.

JOHN SUTHERLAND, 1711

Survey held at Sunderland in November 1840 on the brig *Maid of Athens*. Stem and stern post are composed of English oak, the transoms, aprons, knightheads, hawse timbers of English oak and are fully free from all defects. The floors and first foothooks are composed of English and Stettin oak timber. The other foothooks and top timbers of English oak. The main keelson is composed of American oak and the false keelson of American oak. The deck and hold beams are composed of English and Stettin oak, mostly Stettin. Planking outside: from the keel to the first foothook heads the plank is composed of elm and beech, from the first foothook heads to the light water mark of elm and beech, from the light water mark to the wales of Stettin oak, part ends English oak. The sheer-strake of English oak and plank sheers of English and Stettin oak, the water-ways of pitch pine, the decks of yellow pine.

JOHN BRUNTON, 1840

The tacklings are the forestay, the mainstay;
the tackles, the mizzen stay, the collars, the
main shrouds and chains, the maintop shrouds,
the fore shroud, the foretop shroud, the
swifters, the mizzen shrouds, the top shrouds
and their ratlines, and the parrels to all masts;
the main halliards, the main topsail halliards,
the top-gallantsail halliards, the fore halliards,
the fore topsail halliard, the mizzen halliard,
and the spritsail halliard; the horse, the main
sheet, the main topsail sheets, the main braces,
the main topsail braces, the main bowline and
bridles, the main topsail bowline, the bunt-
lines, the trusses, the lifts, the earring, the
catharpins, leechlines; the robins, garnets,
clewgarnets, ties, martlets.

CAPTAIN JOHN SMITH, 1627

Some of the sailors com-
plained that she had not that
shift of cabling and cordage,
as to the length of her voyage,
and greatness of her burden
was convenient; this being a
thing of all other carefully to
be provided, since all other
necessaries, as they said,
might be borrowed by the
way, but as for ropes, a man
would not impart them to his
own father at sea.

RICHARD MADOX, 1582

There used to be a sail loft, a sailmaker's loft, but an old seafaring skipper, he 'ad seen better times, an' he was a sailmaker in the loft, making ships' sails 'n stitching – no machines in them days. All done by hand. I used to take 'n listen to what he was doing, y'know . . .

Yes. 'Come here, do you want a bit?' I says 'Yes – I want to be a seaman.' 'Come 'ere, sit down here on the bench a little' – a long bench, sails all round, all done by hand, no machine. We used to call 'im Cap'n Roberts. '. . . And mind what you're doin' now, don't spoil a stitch . . . mind what you're doin', and don't move that needle in there. Not too tight! No, that'll do, that'll do.' He said, 'I'll show you a bit of canvas,' he said 'and I'll pull the stitches tight, and see what sort of bloody mess is round that canvas, after the tight stitching.' Oh, it was all wavy, y'know. Instead of bein' nice 'n flat, which was what he were a-doin' – nice 'n flat y'know, but . . . if you pull the stitching tight, . . . in between the stitches . . . goes wavy in the canvas. Aye.

JOHN ROBERTSON, 1971

. . . the sails act upon a ship with reference to her centre of rotation . . . these principles of the wind acting upon the sails, and the water upon the rudder, are the foundation of the whole science of working a ship.

R. H. DANA, 1855

Lead-lines: The hand-lead weighs usually seven pounds, and the hand-line is from twenty to thirty fathoms in length. The deep-sea-lead (pronounced dipsey) weighs from fourteen to eighteen or twenty pounds; and the deep-sea-line is from ninety to one hundred and ten fathoms. The proper way to mark a hand-line is, black leather at 2 and 3 fathoms; white rag at 5; red rag at 7; wide strip of leather, with a hole in it, at 10; and 13, 15 and 17 marked like 3, 5 and 7; two knots at 20; 3 at 30; and 4 at 40; with single pieces of cord at 25 and 35.

The deep-sea-line has one knot at 20 fathoms, and an additional knot at every 10 fathoms, with single knots at each intermediate 5 fathoms. It sometimes has a strip of leather at 10 fathoms, and from 3 to 10 is marked like the hand-line.

R. H. DANA, 1855

Who doubteth but a simple fisherman of Barking knoweth Barking Creek, better than the best navigator or master in this land: so who doubteth but these simple men doth know their own places at home. But if they should come out of the Ocean sea to seek our Channel to come unto the river of Thames, I am of that opinion, that a number of them doth but grope as a blind man doth, and if that they do hit well that it is but by chance, and not by any cunning that is in him.

WILLIAM BOURNE,
1580

The Master and mate are a sort of people who do all by mechanic rule and understand nothing, or very little, of the instruments they use.

SIR DUDLEY NORTH,
c. 1691

I have known within these twenty years that them that were ancient masters of ships hath derided and mocked them that hath been busy with their cards and plats, and also the observation of the altitude of the Pole Star, saying that they care not for their parchments, for they could keep a better reckoning upon a board. And when that they did take the latitude, they would call them star shooters and sun shooters, and would ask if they had hit it.

WILLIAM BOURNE, 1580

As for myself, I will not give a fart for all their cosmography, for I can tell you more about it than all the cosmographers in the world.

THOMAS HOOD, *Pilot*, 1582

Planking a ship is like the skin, sinews and ligaments to an animal.

JOHN SUTHERLAND, 1711

During this storm we witnessed two ships dashed to pieces, and only three hands saved. So completely dashed to pieces were they against the rocks that many persons who came down to render assistance could perceive no remnants of them, except what was floating in small fragments on the sea, or had been thrown on the beach below.

MARY MOLESWORTH, 1830

stem and stern post are of English oak

transoms   aprons

knightheads

hawse timbers

fully free from all   English oak

defects

floors   and first foothooks

are composed of

Stettin oak

timber   other foothooks

top timbers

English oak

main keelson

American oak

false

keelson

American

oak

deck

hold beams

Oak

planking

elm

decks

yellow pine

4
MEANWHILE ON SHORE...

What is all this strange and strenuous activity on an alien element *for*? It is for the purposes of a community which stays on shore. The pure romantic curiosity and explorativeness of man are a real part of it, but it is largely utilitarian self-interest.

If application be made to the merchant, he tells you that merchandising is brought so low, that he can improve his cash in the public funds to much better interest than running hazards by sea. When you come to the owners of vessels, they give you a large account of many thousands of pounds ventured in their bottoms, to no advantage, but considerable loss; if you should at any time accost the masters of ships, they are ready to make a doleful complaint that freightage is now reduced to so low an ebb, that they know not where to go, to get anything for themselves or owners; as for the foremastmen, you may hear them wishing for the increase of their monthly pay, and at the same time, you may observe the poor labouring men bemoaning themselves for want of work.

C. POVEY, 1701

Merchants and owners of ships in England are grown to such a pass nowadays that it is better sailing with any other nation; for when they send a ship out for a voyage they will put no more victuals or drink in the ship than will just serve so many days, and if they have to be a little longer in their passage and meet with cross winds, then the poor men's bellies must be pinched for it, and be put to shorter allowance, so that many times in long voyages men are forced to spend half their wages in buying themselves victuals, but never have any recompense for it. And many other ways a poor seaman hath to keep him poor, one tittle going one way and one another, England being grown the worst kingdom in all Christendom for poor seamen, being abused many several ways, and paying for damnified merchants' goods, they being in no fault of it, and against all reason if things were rightly considered, no other Christian nation doing the like to their poor seamen, but letting them have what they work for, for they earn it with hardship enough yet though they get it with so much trouble and misery yet they spend it with as much joy as they that have a thousand the year, being nobody's foes but their own, their worst fault, not considering of a rainy day.

EDWARD BARLOW, 1663

The first care of parents and guardians, who design to bring up a youth to be a British merchant, should be, to instil into his tender mind the soundest principles of religion and morality, and a sacred veneration for truth; probity should be the basis of all his juvenile actions; nor should he, in his sports and pastimes, ever be suffered to forfeit his word, or evade his promise.

T. MORTIMER, 1772

If the old bitch of a *Betty* had survived the dangers of the sea much longer, I believe she and the master together would have brought me to the parish . . . No more long bills for refitting, no master's long accounts for damage sustained by storm! No, no, if ever they hook the old fool again to make ducks and drakes of his money in salt water, I'll give 'em leave to draw a rope through his guts and tie him to a cable to make a buoy on . . . The merchants are a pack of sharpers, masters of ships arrant knaves, a vessel but a doubtful confidant, and the sea a mere lottery.

E. WARD, 1698

Wee the Subscribers being desirous to be concerned in a Ship & Cargo: both to be about Three Thousand Pounds —— Value to be Employed on a Voyage to East India by Permission of y Seperate Stock allowed by Act of Parliment doe each of us for himself Subscribe for y respective Sums by us hereunder written on y following Condicons. ——

1 That y Ship for this Intended Voyage be a Ship now building at Mr Richard Wells' for Thomas Bowrey one of the Subscribers. ——

2 That Mr Joseph Tolson one of y Subscribers shall be Captain of y said Ship for this intended Voyage and also Supra Cargoe. ——

3 That every person shall before his Subscribing pay Twenty five Pounds p Cent of his Subscription into y Bank of England & deliver such Noate to Tho Bowrey aforesaid for y use of this Intended Voyage. ——

4 That all after payments shall be made as y Majority of y Subscribers shall appoint and any person failing soe to doe shall forfeit his first Payment to y use of y rest of y Subscribers, & any other person may make good such deficiency.

5 That Thomas Bowrey aforesaid and any Two more of y Subscribers who does not goe in y Ship shall have Power to manage all matters relating to this Ship & Cargo. ——

6 That y Subscribers will meet every Tuesday & Thursday at three aclock in y afternoon at y Garraway Coffee house behind y Exchange & oftner as need shall require. ——

7 That Thomas Bowrey aforesaid shall have five Guineas p Cent on y whole amount of y Ship & Cargo in consideracon of his Contracting for said Ship, and advancing his Own Money for account said Ship & appurtenances and also for the Cargoe; and for his Projecting and drawing Instrucons for y Voyage intended, and other troubles in y Outsett of Ship & Cargo. ——

8 That y aforesaid Joseph Tolson shall have ffour p Cent Comission on y Gross Sale of y Cargoe at y Ships returne to England and Ten Pounds p Month Wages wch is in full for all Comission as Chiefe Supra Cargoe, for all Wages as Captain and in Lieu of all Priviledges of ffraight or Private Trade wch he is wholly debarred of. ——

In Wittness whereof wee have hereunto sett our Names and Seales this Twenty ninth day of June in y Year of our Lord Christ One Thousand Seven Hundred & four. ——

Sealed and Deliverd this Paper being duely stampt, In y Presence of

By Tho Bowrey, George Jackson
Tho Hammond & Joseph Tolson

Simon Duncalfe
Isaac Duncalfe

I Tho Bowrey for One Halfe of y aforesaid Adventure ——

I Geo Jackson for one twelfth part of y Adventure

I Tho Hammond for one twelfth part of said Adventure

Jos: Tolson ffor one sixth part off said adven

Elias Grill for one Twenty fourth part of y said

E. Wilson for one twenty fowerth part of y sd Shipp

Elias Dupuy for one twealfe part

There are certain affairs which should be left to the poor, and Common People to enrich them, but there are others which they only can execute which are rich; as that at Sea by way of Merchandizing, which is the most profitable in an Estate, and to the which they should attribute more honour, than some do here at this day. There is certainly no vocation in the which there is so much required as in this; they are not only to encounter, and strive amongst Men, but sometimes against the four elements together.   [C. MOLLOY, 1676]

Ship *Marquis Camden* of London, 1287 tons, Thomas Larking junior, master. Subscribing owners Henry M. Samson of Blackheath, shipowner; Jacob Sims of Sun Tavern Fields, ropemaker . . . Edward Barnard of Rotherhithe, mastmaker; John Mangles, James Mangles and Robert Mangles of Wapping, ship chandlers; Sir William Curtis, Baronet, and R. H. Clark of Wapping, biscuit makers . . . George Enderby of Blackheath, shipowner, and Samuel Enderby, of Paul's Wharf, the legal representatives of Charles Enderby, late of the same place, deceased; William Sims, Sun Tavern Fields, ropemaker.   [ANON, 1820]

This Charter-Party of Affreightment Indented made and Concluded on the Eighth day of July Anno Dei 1731 Between Benjamin Marnes Master of the good Ship or Vessel called the *Charming Nancy* of the burthen of Fifty-five tons or thereabouts, now in the River Thames, of the one part and Joseph Sedgwick of London, Merchant, of the other part . . . for the voyage to Malaga in the Kingdom of Spain . . . accounting always Two Butts of Four Hogsheads of Wine to a Tun, Ten Chests of Lemons to a Ton of Fruit, Eleven Whole Barrels or Twenty-two half Barrels or Forty-four Quarter Barrels of Raisins to a Tun or Ten Barrels of Almonds to a Tun and Twelve pence for every Jar of Raisins . . .

ANON, 1731

LAUNCHING DINNER

		£	s	d
6 lbs sugar at 13½d		0	6	9
	Lemons	0	1	8
	Beef sirloin	0	8	0
4	Lobsters	0	4	6
8	Fowls and 6 Chickens	0	16	0
	Mr Warham the Cook's bill	3	10	6
15	Half Flasks Florence	2	5	0
1	Gallon Brandy	0	13	0
2	Qts. Lime juice	0	2	3
	Porter	0	1	0
		8	08	8
1	Gallon Rhenish	0	6	0
	Boiling the Ham	0	1	0
2	Dishes of Tarts and puffs and Custard and Almond Cheesecake	0	10	0 . . .

CAPTAIN THOMAS BOWREY, 1704

At this office merchants or masters of ships may be supplied with money on bottomry, be recommended to shipping or freights for ships, and have policies, charter-parties and other writing made.

The Mercury or Bills of Advertisements, 1680

PHINEAS PETT, *Master Shipwright*, 1612

Agreement mutually made this twenty fifth day of March Anno Domini seventeen hundred and four BETWEEN Richard Wells of Rotherhithe in the County of Surrey, Shipwright, of the One part, and Captain Thomas Bowrey of London, Merchant of the other part. WHEREIN Richard Wells Doth Covenant that he the said Richard Wells for the considerations herein after expressed shall in good, substantial and workmanlike manner build for the said Captain Thomas Bowrey one good, new and substantial ship to contain the dimensions following:

That is to say in length by the keel from the touch of the sweep to the back of the main post to be sixty three foot and the main breadth from outside to outside of the outer plank to be twenty one foot six inches.

To complete all manner of Shipwright's, Caulker's and Joiner's work as is needful, to find all such iron work as is usual, to find all plumber's, glazier's, carver's and painter's work for the great cabin, forecastle, etc. as usual. To make partitions . . .

ANON, 1704

Old Rope Bought or taken in Exchange.

Quadrants & Compasses made & repaired.

Johnson, Engraver, Hull

NEWMARCH LEE.

Ship Chandler

166. High Street.

HULL.

Late Foreman to Mrs Fletcher.

Paints, Oils, Tar, Pitch, Rosin, Turpentine.

Varnishes, Brushes, Nails, Oakum &c.

William Lem

BROKER,

Sells Ships or parts of Ships by Publick
or private Sale. Lets Ships to Freight.
Enters & Clears Ships at the Custom House.
Makes Insurances on Ships & Merchandize.
Attends at his Office in Exchange Alley, LONDON,
From 9 in the Morning, till 8 in the Evening.
Orders left at his House in Lime Street,
or at his OFFICE,
will be punctually comply'd with.

I. Kirk, Sc. *St Pauls.*

It is well known that immediately on the arrival of a ship of war in port, crowds of boats flock off with cargoes of prostitutes. Hundreds come off to a large ship. The whole of the shocking, disgraceful transactions of the lower deck it is impossible to describe – the dirt, filth, and stench; the disgusting conversation; the indecent, beastly conduct and horrible scenes; the blasphemy and swearing; the riots, quarrels, and fighting, which often takes place, where hundreds of men and women are huddled together in one room, as it were, and where, in bed (each man being allowed only fourteen inches breadth for his hammock), they are squeezed between the next hammocks and must be witnesses of each other's actions; can only be imagined by those who have seen all this. Let those who have never seen a ship of war picture to themselves a very large low room (hardly capable of holding the men) with 500 men and probably 300 or 400 women of the vilest description shut up in it, and giving way to every excess of debauchery that the grossest passions of human nature can lead them to; and they see the deck of a 74-gun ship the night of her arrival in port.

ADMIRAL HAWKINS, 1822

Honoured Sir:

I take this liberty to acquaint you that my husband John Hunter the carpenter of your ship the *Queen* and hath been in her during the course of the voyage for which I have received four month's money of Mr Blackburn and the fifth month was due yesterday. But Mr Blackburn refused to pay me as he wanted an order from you, Sir.

I had a letter from Spithead from my husband dated the 6th and they sailed the 7th. Mr Blackburn desired me to write to you to be so kind as send a letter to Mr Blackburn at North Shields or me at South Shields. Sir, I have five small children and nothing to support them on but what comes from my husband therefore my wants will be very great before your letter comes. A line or two as soon as possible will oblige.

Your humble servant
Margaret Hunter

1794

Snatched from their wives, parents, and everything they hold most dear, inured to the dreadful havoc of war and threatened with every danger of rocks and sands, how can it be supposed, when after having escaped all these dangers and returned to shore, that seamen can command their reason like other men?

ROBERT WILSON, *c.* 1800

The other day, as I was passing along the street, I saw a crowd gathered round an apparently inanimate lump of human clay which was lying down in the gutter. On inquiring what was the matter, I was informed that 'It was only a sailor'! My informant evidently thought that the phrase 'only a sailor' must necessarily explain the condition and location of the lump in the gutter. To him it was the natural condition of the animal; and he would have as soon thought of explaining to us why a pig was in its sty as why Jack came to be there. Yet the man had no intention of speaking slightingly of Jack. Quite the contrary. The phrase was palliative, and not contemptuous, in its tone. Indeed, it is generally used in this sense, for Jack is a favourite with the public. Vices which it does not tolerate for a moment in any other class of men, it pardons in him . . . and the reason is not discreditable to the public. Jack's life is one of hardship, peril and endurance, and demands the exercise of that physical courage, the manifestation of which invariably commands popular favour. Again, he has a reputation for good humour, generosity, and simple-mindedness, and most of his failings are popularly set down to an excess of these estimable characteristics. Of such a man our judgment ought not to be harsh.

HUGH SHIMMIN, 1860

THREE MEN FOR THE

NAVY.

WANTED

For the Townships of Chipping, Dutton,

And Clayton-le-Dale,

THREE ABLE-BODIED

Seamen or Landmen,

To serve in his Majesty's NAVY during the present War only; and as the Time for accepting such Volunteers expires on *Wednesday* next, the 14th of *December*, it is hoped that no True-Born BRITISH TAR will lose so favourable an Opportunity. Such as make an immediate Application will be preferred, and over and above a handsome Bounty, will be entitled to, and receive, Advantages superior to any other Service, viz. The Families and Friends of Volunteers will receive Monthly Pay, and the Volunteers themselves will have a bountiful Supply of CLOATHING, BEEF, GROG, FLIP, and STRONG BEER, also a Certainty of PRIZE-MONEY, as the Men entered for this Service will be sent to Capture

The Rich Spanish Galleons,

and in Consequence will return loaded with DOLLARS and HONOURS, to spend their Days in PEACE and PLENTY.

HUZZA!!!

☞ BOUNTY will be paid by applying to JOHN SWINGLEHURST, of *Chipping*; THOMAS DEWHURST, of *Dutton* ; and JAMES HIGGS, of *Clayton-le-Dale.*

BLACKBURN: J. WATERWORTH, PRINTER.

Everything had been prepared – shot-racks ranged – breechings cast loose – tompions out – gun-tackles coiled down – my friend, the goat, sent down to the cable-tier – the captain's ducks and geese left in the coops, to cackle and quake, and take their chance – the doctor's saws, and knives, and probes, and bandages, and tourniquet, all laid in order, in the cockpit, and I devoutly hoping as, tempted by curiosity, I looked at them, that I might be blown away altogether, rather than that he should exercise his skill on my limbs or carcase.

CHARLES PEMBERTON, c. 1808

Ships Outward Bound;

The *Experiment*, William Gutteridge Commander, 200 tons, 18 guns, 36 men, bound directly for Cadiz, will depart with all convenient speed.

The pink *Adventure*, John Balston commander, 90 tons, bound for Boston in New England, will be ready to take in goods etc. by the 10 instant, and depart from Gravesend with first conveniency.

The *Sea Adventure* of London, John Bloss Commander, English built, 200 tons, 8 guns, bound for Dantzick and Konningsburgh...

The Mercury or Bills of Advertisements, 6 April 1676

Le Tigre, 74 guns	*Alexander*, 74, very bad state
Theseus, 74 guns	*Audacious*, 74, bad state
Cameleon, 18 guns	*Lion*, 64, very bad state
on the coast of Egypt, bad	blockading Malta
state	*Leviathan*, 74
Thunderer, detached off Lorient	*Powerful*, 74
Sceptre, detached off Lorient	*Zealous*, 74 (must go to England)
Acasta, detached off the Saints	at Gibraltar and off Cadiz

Lists of ships in blockade squadrons, Napoleonic Wars

5
GRASP AND VISION

Exploration and discovery are motivated chiefly not by thirst for adventure or dreams of glory but the grasp for gain. But imaginative vision, courage and daring are part of hardheaded enterprise; and occasionally they are the whole of it.

Francis Drake is so boastful of himself as a mariner and man of learning that he told the prisoners that there was no one in the whole world who understood the art of navigation better than he. He also told them that, since he had left his country he had navigated seven thousand leagues and that, to return thither, he would have to sail as many more.

JASPAR DE VARGAS, 1579

What English ships did heretofore ever anchor in the mighty river of Plate? Pass and repass the unpassable (in former opinion) Strait of Magellan, range along the coast of Chile, Peru, and all the backside of Nova Hispania, further than any Christian ever passed, traverse the mighty breadth of the South Sea, and last of all return home most richly laden with the commodities of China, as the subjects of this now flourishing monarchy have done?

RICHARD HAKLUYT, 1589

The three-masted wooden sailing ship was the space capsule of the Renaissance: a self-supporting system capable of taking man into new worlds.
The single-masted square-rigged vessel used to have a hard job doing much more than run before the wind; the three-master can sail against it. She can go where she couldn't go before.

BASIL GREENHILL, 1978

In navigation, none ought to have greater care to be skilful than our English pilots. And perchance some would more attempt, and other would more willingly be aiding, if they knew certainly what privilege God hath endued this island with, by reason of situation, most commodious for navigation to places most famous and rich.

DR. JOHN DEE, 1570

The merchants of London have furnished and sent forth certain ships for the discovering of lands and regions unknown, and have herein deserved immortal fame, for they have showed no small liberality upon uncertain hope of gain.

RICHARD EDEN, 1555

The carrack being in burden by the estimation of the wise and experienced no less than 1600 tons, had full 900 of those stowed with the gross bulk of merchandise. The principal wares after the jewels (which were no doubt of great value, though they never came to light) consisted of spices, drugs, silks, calicos, quilts, carpets and colours, etc. The spices were pepper, cloves, maces, nutmegs, cinnamon, green ginger: the drugs were benjamin, frankincense, galingale, mirabolans, aloes zocotrina, camphor: the silks, damasks, taffetas, sarcenets, altobassos, that is counterfeit cloth of gold, unwrought China silk, sleeved silk, white twisted silk, curled cypress; whereunto are to be added the pearl, musk, civet, and ambergris. The rest of the wares were many in number, but less in value; as elephants' teeth, vessels of China, coconuts, hides, ebony-wood as black as jet . . .

ANONYMOUS SEAMAN, 1592

Voyages of purchase or reprisals swallow up and consume more sailors and mariners than they breed, and lightly not a slop of a ropehaler they send forth to the Queen's ships, but he is first broken to the sea in the herring-man's skiff or cock-boat; once heartened thus, he will needs be a man of war, or a tobacco-taker, and wear a silver whistle – these swaggering captains or huftytufty youthful ruffling comrades, wearing every one three yards of feather in his cap for his mistress' favour, such as we stumble on at each second step at Plymouth, Southampton and Portsmouth. Some of these for their haughty climbing come home with wooden legs, and some with none, but leave body and all behind. Those that escape to bring news tell of nothing but eating tallow and young blackamoors, of five and five to a rat in every mess, and the ship-boy to the tail . . .

THOMAS NASHE, 1598

The principal thing in a pilot or coaster of our coast is to know where he is. By his first soundings his depth will give him light; and as he draws nearer the coast, either of England or Brittany, his depth will lessen, and by his lead he will take up sands by which he shall gather which of the two coasts he is upon, as also if he be shot into St George's Channel. The meanest mariner that trades to Rochelle, Bordeaux, Biscay, Portugal, and Spain, knows more in this kind than the great masters and others that go to the East Indies and long voyages, because they make four or five voyages in and out of our Channel to the others' one, by which they gain daily experience of our soundings, coasts, marks on land, and the entrance of our harbours, which the others cannot do. The skill of a coaster is to know the land as soon as he shall descry it.

SIR WILLIAM MONSON, c. 1625

Fearless our merchant now pursues his gain
And roams securely o'er the boundless main
Now o'er his head the polar bear he spies
And freezing spangles of the Lapland skies
Now swells his canvas to the sultry line
With glitt'ring spoils where Indian grottoes shine
Where fumes of incense glad the southern breeze
And wafted citron scents the balmy breeze.

THOMAS TICKELL, 1713

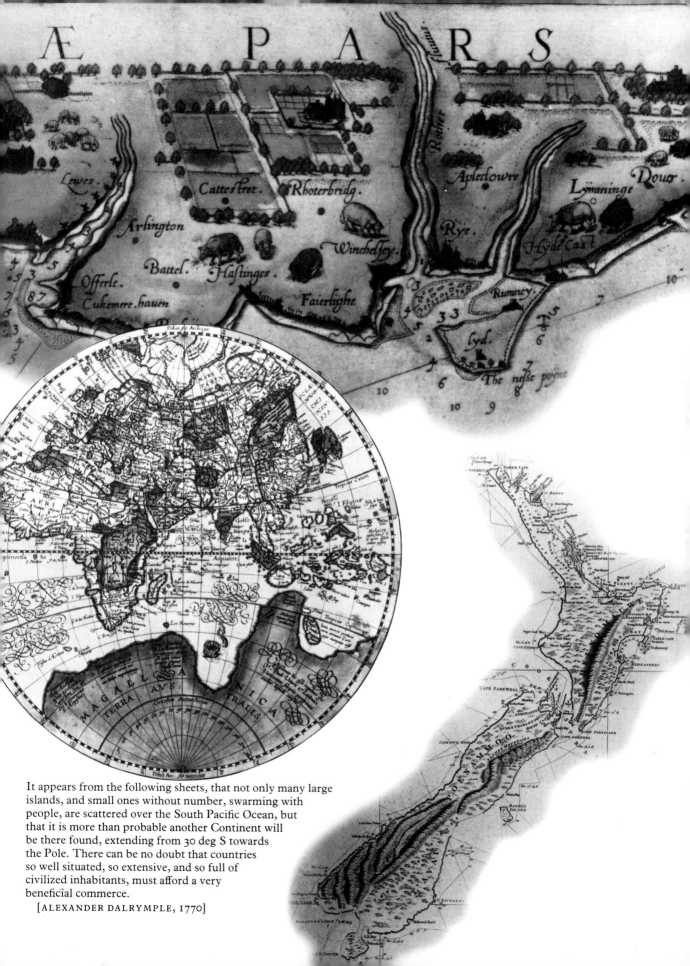

It appears from the following sheets, that not only many large islands, and small ones without number, swarming with people, are scattered over the South Pacific Ocean, but that it is more than probable another Continent will be there found, extending from 30 deg S towards the Pole. There can be no doubt that countries so well situated, so extensive, and so full of civilized inhabitants, must afford a very beneficial commerce.

[ALEXANDER DALRYMPLE, 1770]

Here men were well at morning, and by night frozen to death. It was my fortune to go ashore to get some food, for the allowance of our ship was little, and coming aboard again with my feet wet, and wanting shift of clothes, the next morning I was numbed, that I could not stir my legs, and pulling off my stockings, my toes came with them, and all my feet were as black as soot, and I had no feeling of them.

ANTHONY KNIVET, 1601

The true copy of a note found written in one of the two ships, to wit the *Speranza* (alias the *Hope*) which wintered in Lappia, where Sir Hugh Willoughby and all his company died, being frozen to death.

Sir Hugh Willoughby, knight,
  captain-general of the fleet.
William Gefferson,
  master of the ship.
Roger Wilson, his mate.
William Gittons,
  Charles Barret,
  Gabriel Willoughby,
  John Andrews,
  Alexander Woodford,
  Ralph Chatterton –
  merchants.
John Brook, master gunner.
Nicholas Anthony, boatswain.
Richmond Gwinne,
  George Goiswine, carpenters.
Richard Morgan, cook.
William Light,
  John Brande,
  Cuthbert Chelsie,
  George Blage,
  Thomas Walker,
  Thomas Allen,
  Edward Smith,
  Edward Hunt,
  John Fawkner,
  Rowland Brooke . . .

ANONYMOUS SEAMAN,
1553

The Royal Society have
begun to settle a cor-
respondence through all
countries; and have taken
such order, that in a short
time, there will scarce a
ship come up the Thames,
that does not make some
return of experiments as
well as of merchandize.
This their care of an
universal intelligence, is
befriended by Nature
itself, in the situation of
England. For lying so, as
it does, in the passage
between the northern
ports of the world, and the
southern, its ports being
open to all coasts and its
ships spreading their sails
in all seas, it is thereby
necessarily made, not only
mistress of the ocean, but
the most proper seat for the
advancement of
knowledge.

THOMAS SPRAT, 1667

I whose ambition
leads me not only
farther than any other
man has been before
me, but as far as I
think it possible for
man to go . . .

JAMES COOK, 1774

No people ever went to sea better fitted out for the purposes of natural history, nor more elegantly. They have got a fine library of natural history; they have all sorts of machines for catching and preserving insects; all kinds of nets, trawls, drags and hooks for coral fishing; they have even a curious contrivance of a telescope, by which, put into the water, you can see the bottom to a great depth, where it is clear. They have several sorts of salt to surround the seeds; and wax, both beeswax and that of *Myrica*; besides there are many people whose sole business is to attend them for this very purpose. They have two painters and draughtsmen, several volunteers who have a tolerable notion of natural history; in short, Solander assured me that this expedition would cost Mr Banks ten thousand pounds.

JOHN ELLIS, 1768

Observations of the qualities of his Majesty's bark the *Endeavour*. In a topgallant gale: steers well and runs about five knots. In a topsail gale: six knots. Steers and wears very well. Under her reef topsails, keep her rack full and she goes as well as with whole topsails. The most knots she runs before the wind and how she rolls in the trough of the sea: eight knots, and rolls easy in the trough of the sea. How she behaves in lying to or a try under a mainsail, and also under a mizen balanced: no sea can hurt her laying to under a mainsail or mizen balanced.

JAMES COOK, 1768

Rules to be observed by every person belonging to His Majesty's bark the *Endeavour*, for the better establishing a regular and uniform trade for provisions etc., with the inhabitants of George's Island, and to prevent frauds and disputes as well on the one side as the other.

(1) To endeavour by every fair means to cultivate a friendship with the natives and to treat them with all imaginable humanity . . .

JAMES COOK, 1769

In the harbour our ships were frequently surrounded by swimming natives of both sexes. We often amused ourselves by putting their skill as divers to the test by throwing them glass beads or nails. Some of the older divers and the younger girls rested astride the anchor-cable and were besmirched by the fresh tar with which it had been coated. The men were obliged to go back to their swimming without anybody to help them clean themselves, but I understood that, when it was a question of the fair sex, the boatswain would give them soap and help them to wash.

ANDREAS SPARRMANN, 1773

In the Island of Otaheite, where love is the chief occupation, the favourite, nay almost the sole luxury of the inhabitants, both the bodies and souls of the women are modelled into the utmost perfection for that soft science. Idleness, the father of love, reigns here in almost unmolested ease. What a proportion of spare time must these people have and this leisure is given up to love. I have nowhere seen such elegant women as those of Otaheite; such the Grecians were, from whose model the Venus of Medici was copied; undistorted by bandages, nature has full liberty, and amply does she repay this indulgence in producing such forms as exist here only in marble or canvas.

JOSEPH BANKS, 1769

Nothing but such flights of snow and extremity of frosts, as in all the time of my life I never see none to be compared with them. This extremity caused the weak men in my ship only to decay, for in seven or eight days in this extremity there died forty men and sickened seventy, so that there was not fifty men that were able to stand upon the hatches.

THOMAS CAVENDISH, 1591

Icebergs are beautiful when the sun shines upon them, and lights up their massive forms. We see them imbued with all the colours of the rainbow, and their appearance varies to a most surprising extent. Some are wall-shaped, with flat tops, others rounded and many pinnacled like church spires and Turkish mosques. Terror and beauty combine in this place of desolation. Many a good ship has never been heard of since crossing the Banks of Newfoundland, but if those bergs could speak they would solve the mystery.

CAPTAIN WILLIAM BARRON, 1895

I have quitted any easy retirement for an active, perhaps dangerous, voyage.
I embark on as fair a prospect as I could wish.

JAMES COOK, 1776

Had we lived, I should
have had a tale to tell of the
hardihood, endurance, and
courage of my companions
which would have stirred
the heart of every
Englishman. These rough
notes and our dead bodies
must tell the tale, but
surely, surely, a great rich
country like ours will see
that those who are
dependent on us are
properly provided for.

ROBERT FALCON SCOTT,
1912

. . . I whose ambition leads me not only farther than any other man has been before,
but as far as I think it possible for man to go . . .

JAMES COOK, 1774

6
TRAMPS AND LADIES

After 1880, steam and steel
rapidly take over deepsea seafaring,
though sail persists obstinately in the
inshore world of coastal trade and fishing.
The sailor becomes less of a 'gardener' –
collaborating with forces beyond his
control – and more of a 'driver',
imposing his will in spite of them.

Sail's a lady,
Steam's a bundle of iron!
CAPTAIN BROMLEY, 1964

I was horrified when the crew came on board. They were in a deplorable state, as these sailors often were, joining ships. They were absolutely literally thrown on board onto the deck, the ship was lying at the pier heads, and I said to the Senior Apprentice 'Is that the crew?' and he said 'Yes, they look alright'. Well, we towed out into the Mersey and dropped anchor. Fortunately we were going to get some gunpowder for Valparaiso, and we lay there two days in the river and I used to see an odd figure come out of the fo'c'sle now and then, go under the fo'c'sle head, and go back again, but I still was thinking that they were all drunk, but they weren't. When the day of sailing came and the Mate blew his whistle and shouted 'Square the mainyard!', out of the fo'c'sle came the finest crowd of men you could see, rushing to the braces, throwing them off, shouting and singing and they were a marvellous crew, great crew. Well, actually there were only two British sailors amongst them. The rest were all Scandinavian . . .

CAPTAIN MACLEAN, 1964

I have lived for twenty years in a forecastle, and the men now-a-days will not keep their place clean. No matter how old or small it is, they can keep it clean if they like, but they won't. If it were the finest forecastle afloat, they would be just as bad. If a man is dirty disposed, all the rules in the world won't make him clean, and if he is too lazy to clear his dirt away after him, the only way is to let him lie down in it. If a captain or an officer goes into a forecastle the men think at once that he is up to some humbug, and it does more harm than good.

BOSUN, 1867

The cabin was cosy. It had mahogany panels with a white ceiling, and a decorative skylight in which hung a tell-tale compass and a swing paraffin lamp and the usual barometer and clock. Leather settees surrounded a mahogany table. There was a snug copper fireplace with a mirror above the mantlepiece. The captain's berth led out on the starboard side.

HENRY HUGHES, 1890

To Captain Digby Murray: Dear Sir, when placing the steamer *Oceanic* under your charge, we endeavoured to impress upon you verbally, and in the most forcible manner we were capable of, the paramount and vital importance above all other things of caution in the navigation of your vessel, and we now confirm this in writing, begging you to remember the safety of your passengers and crew weigh with us above and before all other considerations. The most rigid discipline on the part of your officers, should be observed, whom you will exhort to avoid at all times convivial intercourse with passengers, or with each other, and only such an amount of communication with the former as is demanded by a necessary and businesslike courtesy. We must also remind you that it is essential to successful navigation that the crew be kept under judicious control.

ISMAY, IMRIE AND CO., 1871

There were no trimmers on that ship. There were six firemen, and they reckoned to have two firemen on a watch; still, as there was no trimmer, they put one fireman on to the six fires, and one man had to go and trim. They put the six fires on the top of one man. They took two hours at the fires and two hours trimming. I have seen us come up the ladder so exhausted that we had to take the hand-rag in one hand and the sweat-rag in the other to get up the ladder, it was so hot. Even though we signed no grog allowance, they knew the work was so exhausting that they gave us grog both going on and coming off, in leaving London and getting back. I believe that if we had not got that grog some of us would not have come back. For instance, at 12 o'clock, after the watch from 8 till 12, I have seen us lie down on the deck and pant just the same as a whale out of water; lying down for 20 minutes fairly exhausted before we could take a bit of grub.

THOMAS MCCARTHY, 1894

Steam was going back about two o'clock in the morning, and I knew which boiler was short of steam. So I knew who to go to when I went into the stokehole. An' this feller was a Chilean. So I went in and started to tell 'im off – 'Get the steam up!' So he'd just been slicin' the fire, that's poking. An' of course the slice was pretty well redhot by the time he drew it out. Then he made for me with a redhot poker. Well, fortunately the poker was too heavy for 'im, it dropped. An' I put my foot on it. An' then I just went straight at 'im mad, had a good pair of fists in those days. So I just put 'im on his back, gave 'im quite a nice Hallowe'en party.

HENRY CLOW,
c. 1920

A tramp steamer, then, is a vessel of large cargo-carrying capacity and low power of engines, built upon the most economical principles, and run likewise. She goes wherever freight is to be had. The best type of tramp is built and owned in north-east English ports, where the highest shipbuilding science is brought to bear upon the construction of cargo-carriers that shall be at once cheap, roomy, economical, and seaworthy. The lowest type of tramp, on the other hand, is one that is built to sell to the first bidder – built so as to pass Lloyd's surveyor, but without one single item in her equipment that can be dispensed with. Such vessels as these merit all the hard words that have been said of them. Very slow, very unhandy, with dens for the crew to live in and upper works of the commonest material, they are always coming to grief. They are mostly owned by single-ship companies.

F. T. BULLEN, 1900

SS. Tregenna, built 1892, 2623 tons gross:
sailed Penarth for Alexandria, 31st December,
1901; arrived Alexandria, 19th January, 1902;
sailed Alexandria for Constantinople, passed
Dardanelles, 2nd February; arrived
Novorossisk for Gibraltar, 10th February;
arrived Gibraltar, 24th February; arrived
Hamburg, 6th March; left Hamburg for
Penarth, 15th March; arrived Penarth, 20th
March; left Penarth for Piraeus, 27th March;
left Piraeus for Sulina, arrived Sulina, 23rd
April . . .

Seagoing in those days, in sailing ships was a kind of degrading experience, it was degrading in the form of the injustices that were thrust upon you . . . but in spite of these injustices you feel you're one with the ship, she must go. Something gets you in these ships, you find yourself wrapped up, the same spirit as the master's, the ship's got to go and go as hard as you.

SIDNEY RIGGS, 1972

The *Dreadnought* was an up to date ship. She was the first ship where the crew lived aft and on her steam trials she could do 21 knots and when she was doing 21 knots and you were aft down the mess deck she would shake about. Even the ditty boxes would go up and down. She was Flagship of the Home Fleet, Admiral Sir William May and his wife was up there in a yacht. She used to like to see the sailors in Number 5s – a duck suit – and winter or summer she used to like to see the sailors so winter or summer we were always in Number 5s. We used to get up in the morning about half-past five, a quarter to six. We used to fall in on the poop and then away we would go and clean ship, it was in Portland in winter, sanding canvas, holystoning the decks, trousers up to your knees, sometimes for an hour and a half before it got light, and then wash down with the hose. Everything was always wet.

SEAMAN GUNNER STANLEY MUNDAY, RN, *c.* 1907

During the voyage, the boys will curse the ship, curse what they've got to do, complain all the time, but at the end of it, without knowing it, they develop an unspoken, usually, but very deep, feeling of achievement and communion with the ship itself. It's the sort of thing that, if you said it in front of one of those boys, he'd probably strike you, for saying it! They feel it, although they probably don't say it. What struck me was the immense power of a ship which is entirely dependent on the men on her, immense power to demand first of all, very great work, especially in emergency, and to create through that a feeling of oneness among the crew.

ANTHONY HEAD, 1957

Well, the vessel was your own, you were just as proud of the ship as you were of the home, really. Ships used to be kept lovely in my early days, mind, very particular, very particular . . . they were very, very fussy about it in those days, and everything had to be coiled right-handed, you know, you couldn't coil it left-handed, if you were to coil a rope a different way to which the sun were going, the next thing you'd know you'd have somebody's hand under your earhole, and tell you to do the job properly.

CAPTAIN S. RAWLE, 1960

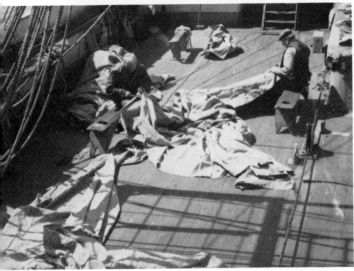

You coaled right up till it's dark and then you've got to sleep just as you are for the night till four o'clock or half-past four the next morning. And so you crawl away onto a couple of coal bags, cover yourself up with some more. You're always, black, dirty; your nostrils, your mouth, everything is full up with coal dust. But you are so tired you can go off to sleep and you wake up in the morning and start off again. You go down for your meals – it's marvellous looking across the table. There were fifty in our mess and two long tables. And all you can see is the whites of their eyes, hardly knowing who you are talking to.

JOINER FIRST CLASS GEORGE CLARKSON, RN, c. 1914

I don't wonder, with all the men lost around the Dogger, we sometimes got human skulls, and that, in the trawl, and more 'an once I've seen a man in oily jumpers, and boots on, shot out on deck with the fish when we've opened the cod end. It made your flesh crawl, shovin' of 'em over again with a capstan bar or your shovels. Lor, the Dogger's a regular ocean cemetery . . .

GREAT YARMOUTH SMACKSMAN, 1909

They were shooting so close that the nets used to touch each other. See, you got to do it, nobody had any sleep, nobody had any anything, all the time it was being hauled, according to the quantity and heavy of them and the difficulty of how the wind was, to get them aboard. About a mile and a half of nets, had all got to be pulled up and every herring pulled out of them. And every bit of that herring had got to be scuppered out into the baskets, and loaded. And you were lucky then, there's a possibility then, after you got them out – off you go straight to sea again. Because time wasn't a factor with them as regards going to sea, they'd go out all hours. If there was a heavy, what they call a shimmer of herring, heavy shoal of herring, well, of course, you'd got to go straight away and haul again. Then you got all that – cycle going round and round and round.

THOMAS WILLIAM CRISP, early 20th cent.

7
SMASHING, BURNING AND DROWNING

Smashing, burning and drowning are what sea warfare, stripped of romantic glamourization, is all about. The heroism and dedication involved are not to be denied; and Nelson himself made the romanticism reality; but the human cost is the most real thing of all.

Those boatswain's mates grinned in the satisfaction of hearing the knots on the rope sink with a dense *thug* into the flesh! If anything more ferocious can be found among wild beasts, I have yet to learn it.

CHARLES PEMBERTON, 1806

When we used to go ashore up Queen's Street, if a Seaman or Stoker went along with *Essex* on his cap, the harlots used to put their aprons over their sterns as a sign of disgust. She was a hot-bed of sodomy.

ENGINE-ROOM ARTIFICER LEGGATT, *c.* 1912

The *Prompte's* crew were like a family united and would, both officers and men, risk their lives to assist each other.

WILLIAM
RICHARDSON,
1799

Her Royal Highness Caroline paid our Admiral a visit on board the *Caesar*. All the girls on board (some hundreds) were ordered to keep below on the orlop deck and out of sight until the visit was over. As Her Royal Highness was going round the decks she cast her eyes down the main hatchway, and there saw a number of the girls peeping up at her. 'Sir Richard', she said, 'you told me there were no women on board the ship but I am convinced there are, as I have seen them peeping up from that place, and am inclined to think they are put down there on my account. I therefore request that it may no longer be permitted.' So when Her Royal Highness had got on the quarterdeck again the girls were set at liberty, and up they came like a flock of sheep, and the booms and gangways were soon covered with them, staring at the princess as if she had been a being just dropped from the clouds.

WILLIAM RICHARDSON, 1805

He waves us to leeward with his drawn sword, calls amain for the King of Spain, and springs his luff! Give him a chase piece with your broadside and run a good berth ahead of him! We have the wind of him, and he tacks about! Tack you also and keep your luff, be handy at the helm, edge in with him, give him a volley of small shot, also your prow and broadside as before, and keep your luff!

CAPTAIN JOHN SMITH, 1627

Two balls struck me; one of them passed through between my fingers and wounded one of them; the other went through my right thigh, and shattered the bone just below the hip. The shock was instantaneous, and for a minute or two deprived me of all sense; the pain I felt was not poignant, but a kind of indescribable sensation, which benumbed me all over. I thought afterwards and concluded from it, that to be shot dead would be a very easy way to be sent out of the world.

GEORGE WATSON, 1812

They have done for me at last, Hardy; my backbone is shot through.

HORATIO NELSON, 21 October 1805

Our ship went right under the four-decker's
stern, and we fired five broadsides into her,
knocked all her counter in, her three masts went
over the side. We engaged five ships at one time,
but they would have sunk us only for the
Temeraire took the fiery edge off us. The
repeating frigate could not see us for fire and
smoke from twelve o'clock until two; they
thought we were sunk, but instead of that we were
giving Johnny Craps their breakfast.

ABLE SEAMAN BROWN,
H.M.S. Victory, 1805

The *Invincible*, my old *Invincible*, blew up, about 6.30. I hadn't my eye on her at the moment. I first saw the crimson gout when it was some hundred feet high, by perhaps two hundred broad. It rose contemptuously, leisurely, at its top, a great baulk of timber or piece of plating, or something, to a total height of some three or four hundred feet. About as high as the Forth Bridge cantilevers, then the red faded out, and there remained blackness below, and a new-formed white billowing cloud above. 18 minutes later, a snow shower of paper leaves fell on us from her. As the black ball drifted away we saw her two ends leaning towards one another, standing on their broken midship section in some 30 fathoms of water. Like some silly fancy picture.

CAPTAIN OSWALD FREWEN, 1916

When we steamed through the patch, the main patch, there was the men on rafts, bits of wood, bravely cheering, waving and there was a smell of cordite, the smell of gas from shells, and also burnt bodies. But unless you were ordered to stop, as you may know, you don't stop to pick up survivors, which is another terrible feeling, and going through this, what I might call the centre of all the destruction, left me with a very nasty feeling inside. I wouldn't say it was a case of being scared, but the thought of all that in the water, a thousand men going down at one go was . . . gave me a queer feeling.

ANONYMOUS SEAMAN, 1916

. . . We rowed away from the ship and she was getting lower in the water and then suddenly her stern started to go quicker under water . . . and then we saw the cat in the water, so we went back 'nd tried to get the cat. The cat'd had kittens not long previously. But anyway he said, 'Better keep clear, Mr So-and-so, you know, she's goin' to create quite a suction when she goes down', 'cause she was over seven thousand ton tramp – so she stood right up on her heels, slowly like that . . . and as she slowly went down, of course, all the smoke and the soot come out of the funnel . . .

FRED PYLE, 1972

Two torpedoes struck us. The ship had broken into two parts, the front part had already gone, taken the majority of the crew with it, hadn't a chance to get out of their beds, only took ninety seconds.

KENNETH COOKE, 1943

The next torpedo come in under there in the bunker. An' how them fellers got out of the stokehole I don't know. The gratins come down on top o' them. The three o' them got out and away, on the deck. A nice lad, a gunner, leadin' gunner – he had an axe in his hand an' when I was goin' down the falls the fall got tangled down below an' they couldn't release it, an' there was heavy sea runnin', sea was swellin' . . . so he cut it, the fall, an' he turned me, lugged me head forward an' I turned out from underneath the bottom an' she goin' away from me, an' she was like a dyin' human bein' – hr, hr, hrr – gruntin', yes.

HAROLD SEYMOUR, 1941

Anyhow, when I hear this bang, de water up to here, the ship is gone! Then next thing I know I see de funnel of de ship. I said 'Praise God' I says, and I heard de fireman down below, I hear him shoutin'. But the engineers, none of them I hear dem. But the only body I hear shout out was the fireman that was down an' below in de stokehole. Well anyhow, I says 'Oh God have mercy, Christ have mercy on me'. And the next thing I know it was goin' down like this, I was goin', goin' an' goin' an' goin', an' I couldn't drown, I say 'Oh God, why can't I drown?' and I shoot straight back up the top.

CHARLIE REECE, 1940

She's a big ship, 10,000 tons . . . she's covered in weeds, shrouded in weeds . . . as the tide comes on the flood and the currents pick up there, the weed lifts from her deck and her rigging and sort of flows with the flood and . . . the whole ship becomes alive; she trembles, and . . . various other movements with her. Parts of her are quite dangerous to enter – well, there's a lot of big conger and a lot of the cargo in the hold, high cargo, is in danger of toppling, and we have to tread with caution going through her but we love her for what she is. She's a wreck, to us, that we've sort of got attached to . . . we treat her with respect, we like her and we know a lot about her. We go down and we look at the engine room and that's just part of where the torpedo hit, and there it is, it's a massive triple-expansion engine, and the valves, you look at them and wonder about the men that controlled them when she was hit back in the War, and you think of these things and . . . you seem to be attached to her in a peculiar way, it's like as if the people are . . . the ship's company still about her . . . she's very much alive on the flood.

SILAS OATES, DIVER, 1967

ADMIRAL LORD COLLINGWOOD, 1750–1810

You will be sorry to hear my poor dog Bounce is dead. I am afraid he fell
overboard in the night. He is a great loss to me. I have few comforts, but
he was one, for he loved me. Everybody sorrows for him. He was wiser
than a good many who hold their heads higher and was grateful to those
who were kind to him. I have been ill lately, and am not recovered from an
odd complaint in my stomach, which is almost a constant pain; I shall
very soon enter my fiftieth year of service, and in that time I have almost
forgot when I was on shore.

ADMIRAL COLLINGWOOD, 1809

Collingwood, in short, take him all in all, will perhaps stand second to
none that ever hoisted a flag. Duties of every kind were carried on with
that calmness and order and regularity and promptitude, which afford a
strong evidence of the directing hand of a master spirit. No swearing, no
threatening or bullying, no starting were to be heard or seen. Boatswain's
mates or ship's corporals dared not to be seen with a rattan or rope's end;
nor do I recollect of a single instance of a man being flogged while he
remained aboard. Was discipline neglected, then? By no means. There
was not a better disciplined crew in the fleet.

LANDSMAN HAY, 1804

There was no doubt that we were under heavy fire, because all round us huge columns of water, higher than the funnels, were being thrown up as the enemy shells plunged into the sea. Some of these gigantic splashes curled over and deluged us with water. Occasionally above the noise of battle we heard the ominous hum of a shell fragment, and caught a glimpse of polished steel as it flashed past the bridge.

REAR-ADMIRAL W. S. CHALMERS, 1916

Two of the boys stationed in the quarterdeck were killed. A man who saw one of them killed afterwards told me that his powder caught fire and burnt the flesh almost off his face. In this pitiable situation the agonized boy lifted up both hands, as if imploring relief, when a passing shot instantly cut him in two. Our men kept cheering with all their might. I cheered with them, though I confess I scarcely knew for what.

SAMUEL LEECH, 1812

Soon after this I heard the roar of the enemy's cannon. A strange noise, such as I had never heard before, next arrested my attention; it sounded like the tearing of sails, just over our heads. This I soon ascertained to be the wind of the enemy's shot.

SAMUEL LEECH, 1812

Arrived in due time at Malta. Each man received as single share six lechins prize money from agent and twelve dollars from captain for prize money on board. Had glorious fun there; those that did go ashore, kicked up what sailors call 'Bob's a-dying'. They hired every horse, jackass and coach, that they could find. They formed themselves into fleets (opponents) and performed several nautical manoeuvres on horseback, which of course must be very diverting. About sixty of the liberty men dined at one inn. At their departure, each took his fork for a spur and lashed it to his heel previous to his mounting. Every sailor (strangers) that they met had a hearty welcome to everything as themselves. We lost one poor fellow by his falling from a high rampart and meeting instant death. For all our mad capers no other person was hurt, excepting a few who were wounded by Venus, in the moment of enjoyment. In short, they were merry and happy while on shore where they could get plenty of liquor (for a seaman's great delight is to wet his whistle when he can).

ROBERT WILSON, 1808

I am a youthful lady
My troubles they are great
My tongue is scarcely able
My grievance to relate
Since I have lost my true love
Who was so dear to me
He's gone to plough the ocean
On board the Victory.

Thirteen of the pressgang
Did my love surround
And one of the accurséd crew
Lay bleeding on the ground
My love was overpowered, though
He fought most manfully
Till he was obliged to yield and go
On board the Victory.

Here's a health unto the Victory
And crew of noble fame
And likewise to the valiant lord
Lord Nelson was his name
At the Battle of Trafalgar
The Victory cleared the way
And my love was slain with Nelson
Upon that very day.

BROADSHEET BALLAD,
The Victory, c. 1805

SIZE, STEEL AND STEAM

The Industrial Revolution goes to sea in iron, brass, copper and coal to replace the 'land and hand' technology of the carpenter, weaver and blacksmith. The complexities are the mathematical ones of curve and equation, the dominant image the 'mobile sculpture' of machinery.

Such, indeed, are the advantages of iron ships over those built of wood, that they only require to be known and understood to be universally adopted, to the exclusion of all others. No wood ships can compete with iron ships in profit or accommodation; and, wherever wood ships are now employed, iron ships may supersede them, and defy competition. I fearlessly predict this to be the case, and that, after a few years, no large wood ship will be built in England, either for mercantile or naval purposes.

MR HOLMES, 1842

The resistance of vessels in the water does not increase in direct proportion to their tonnage.... The tonnage increases as the cubes of their dimensions, while the resistance increases about as their squares; so that a vessel of double the tonnage of another, capable of containing an engine of twice the power, does not really meet with double the resistance. Speed therefore will be greater with the large vessel, or the proportionate power of the engine and consumption of fuel may be reduced.

ISAMBARD KINGDOM BRUNEL, 1836

The wisest and safest plan in striking
out a new path is to go straight in the
direction we believe to be right,
disregarding the small impedimenta
which may appear to be in our way – to
design everything in the first instance
for the best possible results, and
without yielding in the least to any
prejudice now existing, or any fear of
the consequences.

ISAMBARD KINGDOM BRUNEL, 1852

How stands the case when we turn to
iron? Where is the frame, even of the
most intricate form, that our smiths
cannot mould? Where the frame or
beam so large that iron cannot be found
of which to fashion it?

JOHN GRANTHAM, 1842

The essence of War is Violence.
Moderation in War is Imbecility.
You hit first, you hit hard, and keep on hitting.
You have to be Ruthless, Relentless and Remorseless.
It's perfect rot to talk about 'Civilised Warfare'!
You might as well talk about a 'Heavenly Hell'!

LORD FISHER, 1919

Should the head of a rivet break off when the vessel is afloat, it by no means follows that the rivet itself would fall out. On the contrary, when originally secured in a workman-like manner, the piece remains so firm in the hole that it requires the application of a steel drift and a heavy sledge to drive it out. The holes being seldom exactly fair with each other, the rivets swell out and accommodate themselves to the precise shape of the holes, like melted lead run into a mould.

JOHN GRANTHAM, 1842

Forty years ago when I was a laddie the tenement room that our family lived in was only a stone's throw from one of the big shipyards. I could lie in my hole-in-the-wall bed and listen to the drum, drum, drum of a regiment of feet thundering down to the yard. I ate my morning porridge to the sounds of shell rivetters and hand cockers belting away for dear life, a serenade of jazz-time which we used to call Clyde Symphony. Nowadays most of the shell rivets are pushed home by hydraulic power and the rest with pneumatic machines. They still make a noise but it isn't the same noise. It hasn't the rhythm or the character of the old days, when I could beat time with my porridge spoon to the building of a ship.

WILLIE MITCHELL, 1951

The Head Waiter was saying to the steward, 'Now, don't forget I gave you Lord and Lady So-and-so and their family – now, how did they come up?' – and he's got to give so much of that. Then the Head Waiter would have to give so much to the Second Steward for giving the table reservations for the Head Waiter to allot the people these tables, there they're *all* living on each other. Take the deck steward, now, or even a saloon steward – if you wanted something – well, say an omelette – you went straight to the grill cook for that, you see. And if this fellow had not come across at all, the grill cook would – 'Oh!, see to you in a minute', 'n all like that, keep him waiting. Consequence was, when he arrived back at his table – 'Where've you been, steward?' So he had to keep shelling out, to make it run smoothly. That's what disgusted me so much with the Catering Department.

FRED PYLE, 1972

R.M.S. "TITANIC."

APRIL 10, 1912.

LUNCHEON.

CONSOMME JARDINIERE   HODGE PODGE
FILLETS OF PLAICE
BEEF STEAK & KIDNEY PIE
ROAST SURREY CAPON

FROM THE GRILL.

GRILLED MUTTON CHOPS
MASHED, FRIED & BAKED JACKET POTATOES

RICE PUDDING
APPLES MANHATTAN   PASTRY

BUFFET.

FRESH LOBSTERS   POTTED SHRIMPS
SOUSED HERRINGS   SARDINES
ROAST BEEF
ROUND OF SPICED BEEF
VIRGINIA & CUMBERLAND HAM
BOLOGNA SAUSAGE   BRAWN
GALANTINE OF CHICKEN
CORNED OX TONGUE
LETTUCE   TOMATOES

CHEESE.

CHESHIRE, STILTON, GORGONZOLA, EDAM,
CAMEMBERT, ROQUEFORT, ST. IVEL.

Iced draught Munich Lager Beer 3d. & 6d. a Tankard.

R.M.S. "Tartar."—*continued.*

Mr. A. R. Barr
Mr. Thomas
Mrs. Lipman
Mrs. Hele
Mr. Duncan
Mr. De Roos
Mr. Lipman
Mr. Hele
Mr. G. Leech
Mr. H. Robbins
Mr. P. Klein
Mr. J. A. Morrison
Mr. R. H. Fanner
Mr. A. Mitchell
Mr. A. T. Webb
Mr. S. Lurie
Mr. Vorsatz
Mr. B. B. Goodwin
Mr. Bultell
Mr. Andrews
Mr. Volkmer
Mr. R. Glose
Mr. R. H. Nankerois
Mr. Crouch

R.M.S. "SCOT."

Left Cape Town 14th Feb., 1894.

Mr. B. I. Barnato, M.L.A.,
  and Valet
Mrs. Barnato, and Maid
Miss Barnato
Master Barnato
Mr. Woolf Joel
Mr. E. J. Villema
Mr. Maitland
Mr. Hirsch
Rev. Dr. McLeod
Miss Phear
Dr. Spencer
Mr. G. Rock
Mr. Simmons
Mr. Burge
Mr. Lewis
Master Lewis
Mr. Hudson
Mr. J. E. Wright
Mrs. Wright
Mr. Williams
Mr. T. J. Stuart
Mr. Field
Mr. Steele
Colonel Parke
Mr. E. B. de Castro
Mr. C. O. H. Sewell
Mr. Conrad May
Mr. Lawrie
Mr. Duncan
Mr. B. Christian
Mr. C. Slade
Mr. W. White
Mr. Lowenthal
Mr. Lyons
Mr. Douglas
Mr. Spalding
Mr. Dunn
Mr. Adamson
Mrs. Stewart
Mr. Adolf Krant
Mrs. Leyds
Miss Leyds

Whenever a passenger speaks to you you're supposed to answer them, but still carry on with your job, you see. We'll say it's on the boatdeck with the officer on the bridge looking . . . he would see right away if . . . a man was talking or showing people something or . . . making himself rather free – I mean, he'd send one of the quartermasters: 'Tell so-and-so to come up to the bridge' and he'd warn him off then, y'see. Oh yes, yes, you were not allowed to fraternize, of course, and the only people that you would be close to would be the third-class people – now they may have the afterdeck, and you'd see fellows round there trying to talk to these Irish girls 'nd things like that, but in the Cunard Line we had the master-at-arms, there were three or four, now, they used to wander round 'nd they'd tell a fellow, 'You're not allowed to speak to the passengers y'know', 'n 'Now, Miss, you mustn't associate with these fellows', 'nd all like that so . . . I never saw anything going on wrong at all.

FRED PYLE, 1972

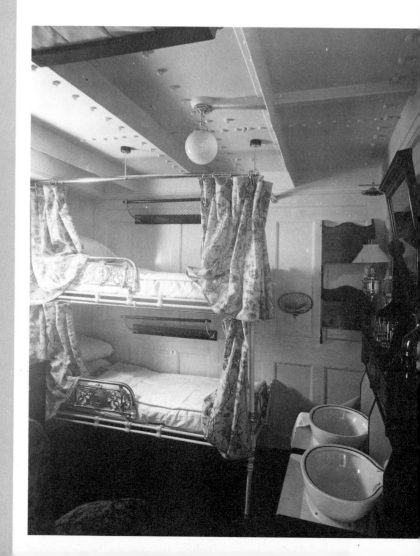

The crank-throws give the double-bass, the feed-pump
    sobs an' heaves,
An' now the main eccentrics start their quarrel on the
    sheaves:
Her time, her own appointed time, the rocking link-head
    bides,
Till – hear that note? – the rod's return whings glimmerin'
    through the guides.
They're all awa! True beat, full power, the clangin' chorus
    goes
Clear to the tunnel where they sit, my purrin' dynamoes.

    RUDYARD KIPLING, *M'Andrew's Hymn*, 1893

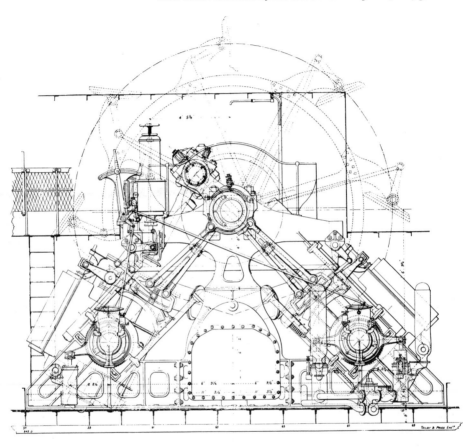

Oh well, I had a notion, of marine engineers since I was a kid. If I went aboard a boat I wasn't content to run about the deck the same as some, I was down below watching. There was one, we had to go from Oban to Tobermory in the boat, you know, and in the old days it was the old compound, oscillatin' engine. The whole engine-room except the platform moved, you see. And I had the opportunity of going down while she was running. And it was this mass of machinery goin' back 'n forward 'n then, when I saw them working the throttle, you see, an' the levers . . . I think, I think the bug got in then.

    HENRY CLOW, 1972

William Gray and Company agree to build and sell and R. Shadforth and Company agree to purchase an iron screw steamer of the following dimensions – length between perpendiculars, two hundred and fifty-seven feet, six inches; breadth of beam, thirty-five feet, six inches; depth of hold to top of floors old style, nineteen feet. To be classed A1 at Lloyds. The main and quarter deck to be of iron. Bridge and forecastle decks to be of iron or yellow pine at purchaser's option. To have Emerson Walker's patent windlass to be worked from the steam winch. The engines are to be by Blair and Company Limited.

    CONTRACT, WEST HARTLEPOOL, 1882

Interdependence absolute, foreseen, ordained, decreed,
To work, Ye'll note, at any tilt an' every rate o' speed.
Fra skylight-lift to furnace-bars, backed, bolted, braced an' stayed,
An' singin' like the Mornin' Stars for joy that they are made . . .

RUDYARD KIPLING, *M'Andrew's Hymn*, 1893

Who comes down the steps but the Chief. A real Chief Engineer, real Scots Chief Engineer, he came from Dunfermline, John Cameron. Stand no nonsense, but very fair. He said, 'The way you stopped these engines an' the way you gave your words of command to the greasers,' he said, 'the way you set that engine away,' he said 'you've handled an engine before.' I said 'Aye, now you're comin' to it,' I said, 'I've handled an engine' . . .

HENRY CLOW, 1972

Well, you never saw much of an engineer in those days, usually, the engineer's quarters and their mess-room were as far from here to that door leading to the engine-room. Or the stokehole, whichever it might be. And they never used to come any farther than that, 'n they never had much to say to each other. They were all elderly men too. Nearly always elderly men.

FRED PYLE, 1972

Now, a' together, hear them lift their lesson – theirs an' mine:
'Law, Order, Duty an' Restraint, Obedience, Discipline!'
Mill, forge an' try-pit taught them that when roarin' they arose
An' whiles I wonder if a soul was gi'en them wi' the blows.
Oh for a man to weld it then, in one triphammer strain,
Till even first-class passengers could tell the meanin' plain!
But no-one cares except mysel' that serve an' understand
My seven thousand horse-power here. Eh, Lord! They're grand – they're grand!

RUDYARD KIPLING, *M'Andrew's Hymn*, 1893

I'll never forget the first morning I went into the Shipyard. Just inside the wicket gates there was a plate, like – and along one of the angle bars some wit had painted the words: 'Abandon hope all ye who enter here'.

WILLIE MITCHELL, 1951

In my early days I was afraid to come to John Brown's because the requirements were so high, and I felt as a tradesman that I might not meet up with what they wanted. So that when I did come in here eventually, I felt an immense pride.

SHIPYARD WORKER, 1967

When the drag chains have been fitted
And they launch the final boat,
There'll be scores of jobless welders
And one redundant poet.

JACK DAVITT, 1977

Walking up the street to my house, I felt I was *the* man. I mean, I was one of the few who was building the *Queen Mary*. You had a great sort of feeling that you were doing something . . . in fact, at that time you were building the biggest ship that was ever built anywhere. I mean, I'm a great believer in being loyal to a firm and I'm very keen on ships.

SHIPYARD WORKER, 1967

9
PARADISE STREET?

The big port of the industrial age was a massive hive of big business, big technology and overflowing material wealth of goods. It had, for the seafarer, a Janus double-face: bewhiskered, knighted and dogcollared respectability, and also the transient paradise of boardinghouse, boozer and brothel; reward and even brief luxury of a kind, and contemptuously rapacious exploitation.

Very, very rough men, very simple sort of fellas . . . well o' course, away all the time, when they come ashore they're like . . . everybody looked down on an old sailor, everybody looked down on 'im . . . one old sailor, he used to get paid off in sovereigns in those days, like, of course, and he'd walk down James Street taking practically all day long to go from pub to pub and at the end o' the day, he'd be broke, and he wouldn't put that money in his pocket, he'd keep it in his hand all the time – I had an old friend of mine, he told me that the one time, money didn't last him the length of James Street, he was broke before he got to the last pub . . .

JOHN TYLKE, 1972

SIR THOMAS SUTHERLAND
Chairman, P & O Lines, 1880–1914

I knew all about that when my shipyards stopped booking orders and began to look like an industrial cemetery – empty berths, rusting cranes and useless stocks. Then for a few years I walked the streets of Glasgow looking for a job and finding a lot of new psychology instead. About a quarter of the male population of Glasgow at that time was keeping warm in Public Libraries – keeping out of public houses, living on bread and margarine, grooming with twopenny haircuts and penny baths and trying to learn something on the side.

WILLIE MITCHELL, 1951

In 1885, when I started in business at South Shields as a shipowner, shipping was in a seriously depressed condition. The rivers and ports of the United Kingdom were crowded with laid-up vessels. I had waited patiently for the opportunity when managers would be forced to sell tonnage at scrap prices. It is more than 99 per cent of a successful deal to buy when prices are low, and sell when they are high. No one ever did or ever will make a mistake by carrying out a policy of this kind – if they can – and this is exactly what I laid myself out to do. By 1895 I was running twenty-five steamers. I devoted long years to the development of the Moor Line, and for over thirty-five years never a day passed without my being either personally, or by letter, by wire or telephone, in communication with our offices. By 1914 we owned forty fine steamers all built to our requirements.

SIR WALTER RUNCIMAN, 1885–1914

What men were doin' for jobs you've no idea. Oh there was ever so many tramped from 'ere to the Bristol Channel, Cardiff 'n Swansea 'n them places. Then the beggars tramped back again because it's no better down there than up 'ere. Oh, dreadful. You could cross this river over ships. Laid up. There wasn't a berth vacant in this river. Right from th' entrance to the bridges. All laid up.

H. BRIGHT, *c.* 1930

The majority o' sailors are very free with their money . . . didn't value money a bit. This is a strange thing. I remember one time, a man went along James Street and he gave out four five-pound notes to various people, the old white fivers, nobody ever found out why, a sailor he was . . . simple sailor, he wouldn't take money away with him to sea . . . No, he wouldn't. I remember a fella, an American, gave me about four or five pound, he said 'I don't want this, I'm goin' away in the morning.'

JOHN TYLKE, 1972

Bacon 'n egg – oh blimey!
That was it in those days,
you know, the first thing a
seaman did when he came
ashore, was to go to a
restaurant: 'Bacon 'n eggs',
right off, that was a luxury.

H. BRIGHT, 1971

I have been in England nearly six years. When I came over I could not speak a word of your language. Now I talk the English well, as well as any, and I go with the British sailor. I am here to-night in this house of dancing with a sailor English, and I have known him two week. His ship is in docks, and will not sail for one month. I knew him before, one years ago and a half. He always lives with me when he come on shore. He is nice man and give me all his money . . . I not spend it quick as some of your English women do. If I not to take care, he would spend all in one week. Sailor boy always spend money like rain water: he throw it into the street and not care to pick it up again, leave it for crossing-sweeper or errand-boy who pass that way. I give him little when he want it; he know me well and have great deal confidence in me. I am honest, and he feel he can trust me. It very bad for sailor to keep his money himself; he will fall into bad hands; he will go to ready-made outfitter or slop-seller, who will sell him clothes dreadful dear and ruin him. I know very many sailors – six, eight, ten, oh! more than that. They are my husbands. I am not married, of course not, but they think me their wife while they are on shore.

SEAMEN'S PROSTITUTE, 1850

Where are we likely to find so great a proportion of public-houses and gin-shops, as in this quarter? or to witness so many instances of beastly intoxication? or to hear language more licentious, and imprecations more appalling? Where shall we find so many brothels of the lowest description? Where shall we find so large a proportion of the voracious and the profligate living on the vices of others, as we shall meet with in such a neighbourhood, battening on the wasteful improvidence, and the debasing vices, of our seamen? Thousands live on their depravity.

REV. JOHN HARRIS, 1837

Oh, loosely living, loosely living . . . you wanted to go down to Custom House, there in Liverpool, and see them pay off, in the days of golden sovereigns, y'know, and the whores waiting outside, y'see, and – ''Ow much you got, Jack?' 'Eight quid.' 'I'll keep you for a fortnight.' 'All right, go on, 'ere you are.' She takes his eight quid . . . and you know, those whores, they used to keep their word, they'd run the fortnight out, you see, then she'd say, 'Now Jack, your fortnight's up, you'd better go and look for a ship', you see, and then he'd probably say, 'Well, what about me grub?' 'Well, that's all right, come back, but go and find a ship.' They played the game, in other words, fair game for the money.

E. L. DAVIES, 1971

On one or two occasions, when we were boarding a tram for the city, several of these Garston girls grabbed us by the coat-tails, attempting to pull us off the tram. They called out to us repeatedly, a touch of significance in their voices, 'Stay in Garston to-night . . . there's plenty of fun for ye here!' As the tram drew off the elderly conductor remarked sagely, 'Them factory girls is as hot as hell!'

NEIL CAMPBELL, c. 1907

W. H. G. KINGSTON
of the Mersey Mission to Seamen

No.	P.C.'s No.	P.C.'s Name	Persons Informed Against	Offence	Date when Sent to Magistrates' Clerks	Date of Receiving the Summons from Magistrates' Clerks	Date of Hearing	Result
1	100A	Morris	Rachel Vinestem	Assist in Management 62 Russell St.	Oct 24 Oct 2	Oct 24	Oct 26 Nov 2 16	adj 7 days do 14 do 40/- P.
2	4 B	Jones	W. Frederick Robinson	Knowingly permit premises to be used as a brothel 35 Edgware St. Oct 22	Oct 27 Oct 27	Oct 27	Nov 2	£5 P.
3	195 B	Ross	Catherine Campbell	Keep a brothel 6 Cadmus St. Oct 23 Nov 6	Nov 7	Nov 7	Nov 9 16	adj 7 days Dismissed Caution P.
4	131 L	Morton	Messrs Morrison Pollenpen + Blair	Ship apprentices without notice to their Master Huskisson Dock 4	Nov 7			*Cancelled*
5	23 B	Lambe	Harriet Johnson	Assist in Management 7 Stitt Street Nov 6	Nov 8	Nov 8	Nov 9	£5
6	23 B	do	Margaret Johnson	Keep a brothel 7 Stitt St. Nov 6		8	8	9 £5
7	do	do	Margaret Roaper	Assist in Management 7 Stitt Street Nov 6		8	8	9 £5
8	109 F	Holloway	Catherine Taylor	Keep a brothel 8 Barnet St. Nov 4/5		8	8	9 £5 P.
9	139 C		Joseph	Keep a brothel 70 Parrl Road Nov 7/9	Nov 10	10	11	£5 P.
10	do		Helena Graham	Assist in management 70 Parrl Road do	10	10	11	£5 P.
					17	17	25	40/- P.
				Nov	17	17	23	20/- P.
						25	30 Dec 14	adj 14 days £5 P.

The Three Admirals
The Grapes and Anchor
The Legs-of-Man
The Neptune
The Gibraltar Vaults
The Dolphin
The Pilot Boat
The Steam Tug House
The Canada Dock House
The Blue Anchor
The Baltic Fleet . . .

The Earl of Effingham, a theatre in Whitechapel
Road, has been lately done up and restored, and
holds three thousand people. It has no boxes;
they would not be patronized if they were in
existence. Whitechapel does not go to the play in
kid-gloves and white ties. The stage of the
Effingham is roomy and excellent, the trapwork
very extensive, for Whitechapel rejoices much in
pyrotechnic displays, blue demons, red demons,
and vanishing Satans that disappear in a cloud of
smoke through an invisible hole in the floor.
Great is the applause when gauzy nymphs rise
like so many Aphrodites from the sea, and sit
down on apparent sunbeams midway between the
stage and the theatrical heaven.

    HENRY MAYHEW, 1850

We came out of the theatre, one of several in the
Liverpool of the early 'sixties, into the cold
drizzle of a December night. In the comparative
warmth and gas glow, amid the dirt, the bare
benches, and sawdusted floor, my shipmate and I
had spent three hours in the ecstatic enjoyment of
an old-time pantomime . . . until the climax was
reached by what we thought were the most
beautiful girls in the world posing in fairy-like
ways. All equally lovely when seen from the
gallery by eyes of youth accustomed only to lean,
unkempt men and empty, restless seas for
months at a time.

    HARRY HINE, c. 1860

They mostly, these little boarding houses, they
all had their own set of men comin' and going,
they treated 'em as one of the family. But the
boardin' house I was connected with, in James
Street, it was what they called a 'hard-up', they
didn't have anybody stayin' there, they only sort
o' used it as a kind of an office . . . the water clerk
who'd arranged the shipping, he'd tell this
boardin' master, we want a crew tomorrow
morning, . . . used to go out, prowl around, he'd
know where to look, and he'd pick up a crew,
been sleepin' out or chucked out or one thing and
another, and about ten or eleven o'clock in the
morning, he'd have enough assembled there for
the crew, he wouldn't have put them up at all.
And he would get a backhander. I remember one
time, that there was two regular soldiers, lancers,
come down to Cardiff here in their uniforms, and
he took them out the back, fitted 'em out with
dungarees, and their uniforms was in the back in
the corner there for months until they got rotted
and thrown away . . . beautiful uniforms, like, I
remember, it was a black uniform with yellow
facings, and pill-box hats. And he shipped them
away to sea as firemen. 'Course, I suppose when
they got away to some foreign port they left the
ship and never got back again.

JOHN TYLKE, 1972

What lunatic architect designed a Merchant Seamen's Home on the exact likeness of a prison, and, constricted by the site boundary, formed the interior to resemble the forepeak of the *Great Eastern*? . . . A narrow iron bedstead supporting a hair mattress, clean sheets, a pillow, two thin blankets and a blue and white counterpane. The size of the room, about eight feet by five, but it was all a seaman really needed for two or three weeks ashore before going broke and shipping out again. I always felt a slight twinge of happiness for the isolation and privacy it gave me, after months in a fo'c'sle full of others.

GAVIN CRAIG, *c.* 1920

And so I began to gather my company abroad, which forced us to search all lodgings, taverns and ale-houses. For some drink themselves so drunk that except they were carried aboard they of themselves were not able to go one step, others feigned themselves sick, others to be indebted to their hosts and forced me to ransom them, one his chest, another his sword, another his shirts, another his card and instruments for sea . . . and others to benefit themselves of the advance given them, absented themselves, making a lewd living in deceiving all, whose money they could lay hold of. Such as go to sea (for the most part) consume that money lewdly before they depart, and when they come from sea, many times come more beggarly home than when they went forth, having received and spent their portion before they embarked themseleves.

SIR RICHARD HAWKINS, 1603

The shipowners at the several ports of the United Kingdom have felt it necessary to give seamen engaged for their ships an advance for every voyage of not less than one month's wages, to enable them to pay debts contracted for board and lodging ashore while waiting employment, and for the purchase of clothes and outfit requisite for the voyage. This is done, not by a money payment, but by an advance note. The seamen endorses and gets this note discounted, sometimes by the keeper of the boarding-house, at other times by the clothier or dealer who supplies the goods, the discounter deducting 2s. per pound discount, and the amount due to himself for the board and clothes.

JAMES O'DOWD, 1873

When I was a schoolgirl I sailed with my father in a schooner called the *Cambridge*, belonging to Inverness. We spent our school holidays there year after year. On one occasion we were seven days off Cape Wrath because it was so stormy and the wind dead ahead, we couldn't take her in. So I will always remember the lighthouse on the headland and the sea breaking on these fangs of rocks below, and every now and then Dad would shout out, 'Stand by, About ship, boys!' Round she would come, sails flapping, sheets walloping, and fetch back to Lewis again. About ship again, keep round, until I was just sick of it. In fact we could have reached America, we were that often back and forth on that run.

MRS FINLAYSON, 1964

When they first joined a ship in harbour they would have a day or two to find their way around. We would take them aloft in harbour first a little way up one side, and them to the crosstrees and then over the crosstrees and down again. At sea, they would not be allowed aloft at all at first, but soon they would be riding down the topsail in bad weather. A small boy was given special jobs to do. Outside Appledore bar in the early morning there was often a south-westerly breeze off the land which did not last very far out to sea. I have often anchored on a still night off the bar and told the boy to wake me as soon as the land breeze made. And then about four in the morning I would hear him shout, 'I can smell the hay coming off the land, master!'

WILLIAM SCHILLER, *c.* 1910

10
SEAPOWER

The awesome power of the sea has always exacted a high casualty rate from those who used it; and seafaring has also been prolific in 'industrial accidents' of all kinds, from saltwater boils and ruptures to crushings and maimings. Today losses are negligible compared with those of the era of sail; but the sea is still one of the most dangerous occupations.

She says, 'Did you hear the wind, did it keep you awake last night?' I says, 'No'. And then she says, 'Wait until your sons go to sea, you won't sleep the same,' and it was true.

MRS GRACE HOLLAND, 1971

Dear friends, When you find this, the crew of the ill-fated ship *Horatio*, Captain Jackson, of Norwich, is no more. We have been below for six days. When I am writing this, I have just left the pumps, we are not able to keep her up – eight feet of water in the hold, and the sea making a clean breach over her. Our hatches are all stove in, and we are all worn out. I write these few lines, and commit them to the foaming deep, in hopes that they may reach some kind-hearted friend who will be so good as to find out the friends of these poor suffering mortals. I am a native of London, from the orphan school, John Laing, apprentice. We are called aft to prayers, to make our peace with that great God before we commit our living bodies to that foam and surf. Dear friends, you may think me very cool, but thank God, death is welcome. We are so benumbed and fatigued that we care not whether we live or die . . .

JOHN LAING, 1860
(Message washed ashore in a bottle on the sands of South Shields)

The hurricane raged with the most tremendous violence. Every succeeding wave as it approached us with its towering curling summit whitened with foam, looked like a huge mountain with its top enveloped in snow threatening to overwhelm us.

LANDSMAN HAY, 1809

New Brighton, the well-known watering place on the Mersey, was a scene of great excitement, in consequence of a large portion of the cargo of a brig which had been wrecked on the previous day, having been washed ashore near that place. Many of the rum casks had been 'tapped' before they fell into the hands of the coastguardsmen, and the drinking of the raw rum caused a scene of debauchery totally indescribable. All through Tuesday night and Wednesday morning, men and women, and even children, were found in a state of unconscious intoxication among sandhills. More of the bodies of the crew of the ill-fated brig have been recovered.

NEWSPAPER REPORT, 1866

You never knew what you was going to get in the trawl. And on one particular occasion we were hauling the trawl, and when you used to haul the trawl you used to have to pull the net in with your hands. And this particular case we're hauling up and every time you hauled in you'd look over the side, see if you could see anything. Then just haul again, then look over the side. So of course, when the cod end was nearing the top, looked, hello, what we got here? Bladder of lard. Floating on the top. Inside the cod end. Up – up she come again, pull up, looked – again, oh good God, you say, that's a man. And the bladder of lard we saw was his bald head. Of course we – hoisted him up, on the deck, let him down on the deck, gently, laid him out, and we could see – he was a fisherman. A Lowestoft fisherman by his clothes, his jumper, his boots, and everything, we could see – but we never heard of anybody being lost, until Sunday, we spoke to a fellow – coming out from sea, or coming from Lowestoft on the Saturday, we spoke and we said, have you heard anything – about – anybody being lost? He says, oh yes – Jolly Bob Adams. He's lost off a smack called the *Deal Greatest*.

THOMAS WILLIAM CRISP, *c.* 1910

Over-insurance is another of the sometimes sources of danger; and that this arises, and can only arise, from downright wickedness, no one can fail to perceive. We hear of instances continually where a man induces the underwriter, by falsehood and fraud, to take some hundreds of pounds of his money per annum from him more than is necessary to fully insure him against the utmost possible amount of his loss in the event of shipwreck. Now, a man in business who lays out money, does so with the expectation of getting it back, and with a profit; but in this case he cannot get a profit – he cannot even get his bare outlay again, or any equivalent for it, except in the event which it is an insult to anyone's judgment and common sense to ask them to believe he did not actually take measures to bring about – that is, the wreck of his ship.

SAMUEL PLIMSOLL, 1873

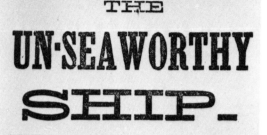

THE
UN·SEAWORTHY
SHIP.

MANCHESTER :—T. PEARSON, Printer, 4, and 6, Chadderton Street,

Copyright.

Written by J. SMITH, *Denholme, near Bingley.*

AIR:—DRIVEN FROM HOME.

THE doomed ship weighs anchor, out she's bound,
With cargo too heavy, and timbers unsound,
A storm overtakes her, reef! reef! every sail,
But all to no purpose, she's lost in the gale;
See the old vessel, now tossed on the waves,
Telling her crew, to prepare for their graves,
Sent out insured, with a hope she'd go down,
Not caring for widows and orphans at home.

Chorus :
Honour to PLIMSOLL, his labour will save,
Thousands of brave men, from watery graves,
May his movement, all our support adorn,
For his work will save thousands of lives, yet unborn.

Out on the wild waves, sailors must go, [know,
Earning bread for their children, what perils they
In old rotten crafts, which ship agents procure,
Brave men they are lost, in those vessels insured
The Captain is anxious the vessel to save,
From the tempest, who threatens a watery grave,
But all human efforts, can't keep her afloat,
Oh, God! she is sinking, out! out! with the boat

Down with the life boat! out on the waves,
Hoping to find land, or sight some vessels sail,
They pray to be saved, but what can they do,
Surrounded by wild waves, that boat and her crew
The storm it is raging, the billows they roll,
No help it is near, for to save those poor souls,
The boat is upset, that brave crew is lost,
This, this, is the price, which our rotten ships costs

Out! out! ye lands-men, out with a will,
Stand up in Justice, for *Plimsoll's Great Bill,*
Don't be rejected, its on God's mission sent,
But up, all as one man, before Parliament;
The Nation demands it, 'tis the widows cry,
The sailors, poor orphans, we can't pass them by,
Let us work every soul, to help brave *Plimsoll* through,
And then we may boast, of our ships & their crews,

774

During this storm we witnessed two ships dashed to pieces, and only three hands saved. So completely dashed to pieces were they against the rocks that many persons who came down to render assistance could perceive no remnants of them, except what was floating in small fragments on the sea, or had been thrown on the beach below. We could distinctly see the distracted countenances of the poor sufferers as they clung to the rigging, their faces turned to the rocks on which their ship was dashing; every wave covered the greatest part of the ship, striking from the deck the sailors on board, each wave leaving still fewer, until the strength of the strongest gave way to the force of the water, and the ship was soon after dashed to pieces.

MARY MOLESWORTH, 1830

The ship was grounded on Hammonds Knoll, and the only thing we could see were her mast, her funnel and the bridge. Everything else was under water. And great seas breaking on her starboard side and across her and round her, and round her stern, and round her bow, and meeting on her port side, and thrown up into the air all of sixty or seventy feet.

'SHRIMP' DAVIES, 1941

All you could hear was the sea crashing over the ship. Then the moon went down, so we knew it was getting late, it got dark. You could hear great grinding noises underneath and bits coming apart, and when they came apart it was just like somebody tearing, say, the Forth Bridge down.

WILLIAM HICKSON, 1941

Once, so huge a sea brake upon the poop and quarter, upon us, as it covered our ship from stern to stem, like a garment or vast cloud; this source or confluence of water was so violent, as it rushed and carried the helmsman from the helm, and wrested the whipstaff out of his hand, which so flew from side to side, that when he would have seized the same again, it so tossed him from starboard to larboard, as it was God's mercy it had not split him. It grovelled us on our faces, beating together with our breaths all thoughts from our bosoms, else than that we were now sinking. For my part, I thought her already in the bottom of the sea.

GABRIEL ARCHER, 1610

In the old days a lot of seamen didn't swim on principle, they wouldn't learn to swim because if a chap fell overboard a lot of skippers won't stop for him, because if they were running afore a strong wind, it might be a gybe . . . the sail of the mast would go out over and they'd lose more men trying to pick up one . . . so they'd say, well, one's gone, let's leave it at one, and that chap drowned, so it's better to drown than just swim about and drown later on. So they didn't learn to swim on principle.

BOB ROBERTS, 1967

Sometimes it didn't even look like water at all. Odd green cliffs, tremendous pyramids that fell. And then all I knew was a terrific shout from the mate – 'Look out!' And what looked like a great cliff loomed up to starboard and . . . well . . . the next thing I knew I was being rolled about – cleared the boat – . . . Ah, it was a very odd sort of feeling of being slightly suffocated and then looking up into a long green spiral of glass.

BILL SMART, c. 1920

There was two trawlers got caught in a storm and they were fairly well up north anyway, and the wind was hurricane force – northerly. The only thing they could do was dodge into the wind, which is steering very, very slowly into the wind – . . . soon as they turn around they'd have tipped over . . . and they got into freezing fog and they started to ice up, and of course the further north they went the colder it got, and the more they iced up . . . and that was that. They tried hard to clear the ice, couldn't beat it, and the skipper got everybody up on the bridge and into the radio room – they were in contact with the U.K., and they all had telephone calls home. Said goodbye, and eventually were just turned over and were lost. Nothing anybody could do about it. Everybody knew where they were, everybody knew what was happening . . .

RICHARD SHENTON, 1979

The same Monday night, about twelve of the clock, or not long after, the frigate being ahead of us in the *Golden Hind*, suddenly her lights were out, whereof as it were in a moment, we lost the sight, and withal our watch cried, the general was cast away – which was too true. For in the moment, the frigate was devoured and swallowed up of the sea.

EDWARD HAYES, 1583

I spoke to one of the trawlermen who had been out there when one of the ships was lost and he said they were all fairly close together and one of the dots just disappeared off the radar . . .

RICHARD SHENTON, 1979

We found ourselves encompassed about with Ice . . . All this day, we did beat, and were beaten fearfully amongst the Ice, it blowing a very storm. In the evening, we were inclosed amongst great pieces, as high as our poop, and some of the sharp blue corners of them did reach quite under us.

THOMAS JAMES, 1631

From the casualty list of the *Titanic*

JOSEPH BELL
Chief Engineer

W. E. FARQUHARSON
Senior Second Engineer

NORMAN HARRISON
Junior Second Engineer

ARTHUR J. ROUS
Plumber

WILLIAM DIXON MACKIE
Junior Fifth Engineer

WILLIAM KELLY
Assistant Electrician . . .

My heart is very sore for the engineers of the lost *Titanic* . . . Though a sailor from my earliest youth, I have always felt the most full-souled admiration for the men of fire and steel and steam who, far, far down in the bowels of the great ship, keep the motive power going while the Parisian café, the restaurant and all the gorgeousness far above their heads is in full swing providing their pay. I confess that to me one of the most touching facts yet elicited in the course of this great story, this epoch-making tale of the sea, is that all the lights were shining when she went down.

FRANK T. BULLEN, 1912

The Cromer boat had a great
big swing right alongside the
ship, great big hooks come
aboard there, one of these old
Norfolk voices bawls out,
'Come on lads, let's get out of
it'. And the Captain says 'All
right lads, abandon ship'. And
you know, I felt sorry for them
when he said that. You know,
'cause we clattered down these
old ladders, fell into the
lifeboat, we didn't trouble to
get in it, we just fell in,
whichever way you got in you
got in, if you went head first it
was the same, they'd catch you
at the bottom.

WILLIAM HICKSON, 1941

I'd heard people say that death by drowning is a pleasant death, but it's not, it's terrible agony, and you're sort of gasping for breath and wanting to finish it. And I did in fact stick my head in the water . . . Then I thought, well, I must have another gasp of breath, and opened my eyes and there's the lifeboat . . . and I'm shouting to them, I tried to shout to them 'Come on, you buggers', you know, and I had a feeling of pride that this thing is still upright . . . and I see my brother, my eldest brother, come out from the canopy and come along the deck and take the rope from somebody else, that they were preparing to throw to me and I could see him coil it in his hand, and I knew in my own mind that it seems that if I had been a mile away he would have reached me with this rope. I saw the boat go up on the sea and run away from me a bit and I knew that he was waiting for that and when he got the maximum height that he could get the rope would come and it dropped right on my chest, four or five lovely big coils you know, and I wrapped a turn round this hand and a turn round that one, and in my teeth as well, and they were pulling me in and then another sea broke either side and I felt she would come towards me and push me under again and I stuck my foot out they pulled, and I hit the side, and they kept pulling, and I was on board.

'SHRIMP' DAVIES, 1941

Moving in fascination over the deep sea he could not enter, man found ways to prove its depths, he let down nets to capture its life, he invented mechanical eyes and ears that would re-create for his senses a world long lost, but a world that, in the deepest part of his subconscious mind, he had never wholly forgotten. And yet he has returned to his mother sea only on her own terms. He cannot control or change the ocean as, in his brief tenancy of earth, he has subdued and plundered the continents.

RACHEL CARSON, 1951

11
'REVOLUTION?'

Since the fifties and sixties, an
accelerating technology has overwhelmingly
transformed the life, work and conditions of the
seafarer. Machinery and electronics have demanded new skills
and training: and the appalling conditions and
brutal discipline of the past are no longer
possible if men are still to be got to sea. Yet the sea
still remains an element to which man
can return only on its own terms.

And these old ships, in my early days, they had
great big square-headed topsails, you know,
great big yards to them. Used to have to go up
and ride these blooming things down, you know,
to tie 'em in. Little bits of boys, like, you'd billow
out on these sails . . . well, I can't understand
why you didn't get blown away off o' them. The
wages were very small, but ships, there were
ships galore. I don't know, nowadays it gets on
your nerves to look out 'ere. We're looking
across the water now, there's not a ship in sight,
no ships at all. But years ago, whiles, there was
ships, ships, that's all you seen. I suppose really,
the thing was, they were all-sails ships and they
didn't get about so fast as they do today – today's
the tendency to carry larger cargoes in ships,
isn't it, really, make a quick do of it, that's how
it is.

CAPTAIN S. RAWLE, 1960

Well, when I first got my
ticket I was like any other
young man, dead keen, I
would have gone to sea on
a plank with an engine on
the end of it.

FISHING SKIPPER,
PETERHEAD, 1979

Over 20 years – everything's modernised, stays in port are much shorter, ships are faster, more modern, equipment more sensitive to vibration and sea air, electronic equipment, get trouble with 'vibes'. Conditions are wonderful now, most modern ships you have your own toilet and shower and you all live in little self-contained flats. Food all provided. Bed linen washed – you only have to do your own personal washing, get a bit of a lord, stewards bring you tea in the morning – chappy who first goes to sea thinks he's got it made – as long as you don't get too bigheaded about it – like Lord Muck and look down on the stewards.

STUART JAMES MURDOCH, *Electrician*, 1979

When I first went to sea – it was 1937 – in those days seamen seemed more dedicated to their jobs. I suppose it might have been because there wasn't so much work ashore for men, so when they had a job at sea they took it as their livelihood, but now a lot of the young fellows at sea sort of use it as a stopgap. All they look forward to is going abroad, to different places, ports. They don't seem to take the industry seriously. They've changed. Radically changed.

HENRY HUTCHINS, *Bo'sun*, 1979

In the docks in Cardiff here when I was a kid I always used to watch the ships coming in and my father used to go to sea, and, well, my brothers, none of them would entertain the thought, but I like it. I have worked ashore on and off but it's something that gets in your blood and you have to go back again. I couldn't settle down in factories and places like that. I tried it.

H. CARTER, AB, 1979

Not so much of the old traditional skills, mostly gone now, all the fancy work, all you did on deck manually, all gone now, you've got all this sophisticated gear, cargo-handling gear, cranes, the modern sailor is more of a technician than a sailor, it's not a man today who can run around with a marlinspike in his hand, it's a man who can handle tools, burn and weld, do all the odd jobs. It's a good all-rounder, that's what you need at sea today.

JAMES PACK, *Bo'sun*, 1979

I went to sea in the summer of '72. I did a four-year apprenticeship, at the end of which I took OND Second Mate Certificate . . . I did one trip on a cargo ship as Third Mate, and another trip as Second Mate on a bulk carrier. And I came up home to do my Mate's Certificate . . . I think I've had every kind of reaction you can imagine . . . sometimes you get the crewmen think the world of you and they'll do anything, and some of them just won't do a thing unless you absolutely kick them around . . . And that goes for the officers as well, and the captains – some of them, the thought of having a woman on the ship brings them out in purple spots, and so they make life as desperate for you as possible and they make everything a real pain. But then there are captains who are absolutely marvellous and think women at sea are the best thing since sliced bread . . .

NINA BAKER, *Second Mate*, 1978

Today, you've still got the natural hazards. The weather, which has always been the seaman's worst enemy, I mean you can't control the weather but in some cases it's more hazardous going to sea now than what it was years ago, 'cause you've got so much sophisticated equipment and if you've got untrained people you're liable to have a lot of accidents. Another thing is these chemical tankers carrying all sorts of weird and wonderful things that the scientists know about, they know what they do, and what they're for, but they don't know the effect on the human body and it's causing quite a lot of seamen a lot of concern. We don't know what we're sailing on and the fumes of some of them are really deadly.

JAMES PACK, *Bo'sun*, 1979

Moving in fascination over the deep sea he could not enter, man found ways to probe its depths, he let down nets to capture its life, he invented mechanical eyes and ears that would re-create for his senses a world long lost, but a world that, in the deepest part of his subconscious mind, he had never wholly forgotten. And yet he has returned to his mother sea only on her own terms. He cannot control or change the ocean as, in his brief tenancy of earth, he has subdued and plundered the continents.

RACHEL CARSON, 1951

A diver is someone who likes the water, who's lived in the water or on the water most of his life and it's still his hobby.

DAVE FAIRBROUGH, *North Sea Diver*, 1979.

It's more or less just love of water. Being under it or top of it doesn't make that much difference. I think it's just working alongside the water. Being underwater, you can see it's very attractive when you're in shallow water and there's a lot of colour in the sea. But as far as the oil rig working you're not actually seeing much, you're just down there doing a job. I think it goes back to this love of the sea. You don't think you're working under the water, just in the water. I think it's most divers do it for their hobby. That they get paid is an extra incentive.

BILLY MACLEOD, *North Sea Diver*, 1979

. . . And the ragged rock in the restless waters,
Waves wash over it, fogs conceal it;
On a halcyon day it is merely a monument,
In navigable weather it is always a seamark
To lay a course by: but in the sombre season
or the sudden fury, is what it always was . . .

    T. S. ELIOT, *The Dry Salvages*, 1943.

You'll always have the elements to
contend with. Over last Christmas so
many ships went down because of bad
weather and the crews were all lost.
That's one thing will never diminish.

    HENRY HUTCHINS, *Bo'sun*, 1979.

. . . a sea that was a boiling mass of fury –
I've never in my life seen such seas.
Indeed, today when I go over it in my
mind I get terribly frightened. Well, the
coastguards told me afterwards that we
went alongside ten times – *I* would never
know. And there was one man still on
that ship, and somehow or other I
couldn't leave that man. I took another
desperate gamble, drove the lifeboat in
again, and this time she was lifted right
on top of the ship. Well, if she would
have touched the ship not only would we
have been drowned, we'd have been
smashed to bits in that terrible sea . . .
To my amazement, this man was
sprawled on the deck. Two of the men
managed to drag him to safety . . .

    COXSWAIN RICHARD EVANS, 1979

A lot of couples, they meet on board ship and they'd like to get a cabin together, sometimes it's allowed and sometimes not, 'cause there were a few problems – where the girl and boy would have arguments, they might break up and then you'd have to split the cabins up, shuffle them around. If they get a cabin, they make it. It's not looked down on or brushed aside like ashore – it's just accepted. You do what you want to do – if nobody likes it, well, tough. I like the fellas, much prefer them. I wouldn't trust them – no way. They live their lives, you live yours and if you eventually get married, well, fair enough, but I wouldn't trust them, not if I was ashore and

You do get funny instances, like when you have a master and the engineer want the stewardess to live with them, then the ship runs much worse than if it's one of the crew living with a stewardess. When I confronted that particular situation, I was a mate on the ship, and the bo'sun was living with one of the stewardesses, and I could find no fault in his work or anything – no problem there, but I was assured later on in the voyage by the stewardess that the man living with her did a better day's work with her than if he wasn't living with her, so I think it's probably right and they're a lot more contented than the single man. So there is something in it. Although life revolves around the bars a lot, there is this

It has changed, quite right, it's much more sensible discipline now, I think we rely much more on a sensible self-discipline, discipline by consent is the OK phrase I think – whereas in the old days, if a laddie stepped out of line you whoofed him round the ear, it's much more a case of education now and training the chap in the right direction. The big question, I think, is whether the discipline will stand up to the absolute stress of an action situation. I don't think this has ever been proved in recent years and remains to be seen.

LT.-CDR., RN, 1979

I think a naval wife does require to be a fairly resourceful person, in much the same way as somebody running a one-parent family. I think, too, she has to be quite capable of running her life without reference to her husband. That I don't think is necessarily very difficult. What may be much harder is running her life with reference to her husband, when he comes home. Oh yes, of course there are enormous advantages. The social life one gets is far more varied than I think one would normally find in civilian life, and certainly far more varied than one would find in civilian life at the same socio-economic level. I have ranged, for example, from a Buckingham Palace Garden Party, invited purely because my husband was in the Navy, to an entertaining evening in a Singapore brothel. I don't think I would have qualified for either of those if I hadn't been married into the Navy.

NAVAL WIFE, 1979.

Yes, I think in this modern day and age, with the destructive power of modern weapons, you require very much centralised control in the end, otherwise things could get out of hand very quickly, which is totally unintended, if a commanding officer goes off doing all the things by his own initiative.

COMMANDER, RN, 1979

For me the main attraction was
undoubtedly the race itself. It
was simply a great adventure in
which you had to pit your wits
and your skill against the sea. To
go singlehanded was to add to
the satisfaction and feeling of
achievement – once you had
arrived. There were risks, of
course; from collision with a
ship, an iceberg, or some large
jetsam; from illness or accident;
from falling overboard, or from
excessively bad weather. But
many sports involve risk, and
certainly an adventure is no
adventure without it. I had now
to decide whether the loneliness,
the sheer discomfort and the
likelihood of being frightened a
great deal of the time were going
to be worth that nice feeling of
achievement I hoped to enjoy
after the finish. Looked at from a
rational point of view I should
probably have stayed at home,
but somehow I always knew I
wouldn't.

CLARE FRANCIS,
Yachtswoman, 1977

You're away from troubles such
as politics and wars and
accidents. You're not getting
battered by it all the time.
You've got a telly on board ship
but you never listen to it. Papers
you only get now and again, but
really you're kept very well away
from the troubles of the world.
We do have a station on board
the ship which does give us a bit
of information about what's
going on, but that's it. Apart
from that you're completely free
of it.

STEWARDESS, 1979

Well, there's more comradeship. All mix in together, the officers and the crew. You get some bad ones, but mostly we're all mixed in. You've got more contact. It's only a small ship, 8 or 10 men all mixed in. Go ashore together. But the deep sea, they all keep to their separate parts – mates, engineers, sailors, catering. But with the coasting you're in a small group – it's like being at home really – so you get mixed in.

J. MCGRANN, *Ship's Cook*, 1979

These large VLCCs running between the Persian Gulf and the UK and Northern Europe, they're at sea for 42 days, and the big moment is when the films come on board at the Cape, when they arrive in the Persian Gulf and when they arrive back in the UK, that's all, there's nothing in between, there's a blank, in effect, they try and fill with the movies and games of squash and swimming pools and all the rest of it . . . the more demanding type of man doesn't want to be marooned on a large ship for six weeks at a time with three points where he has to exercise some ability and some skill, you know, his skills are not used, whereas a man on a small coasting ship running around the North Sea is using his ability all the time, and he's happy, and he's a much better seaman because of it.

MARTIN LEE, *Pilot*, 1979

It seems to be a case where you gradually build up a basis of good crewmen. It never ceases to amaze me why the good ones should stay, because the job is nothing like being a deep-sea sailor, painting and chipping, but they seem to like it. They seem to like working up to their waists in water sometimes, the rougher it is very often the happier they are – afterwards – not at the time – afterwards; this magic word 'sense of achievement' comes in, I suppose.

CAPT. L. HARRISON, 1979

All in all for the crew in general the life has become a good bit easier, although the actual labour is much about same. The labour of handling fish, stowing fish and icing fish has never changed, didn't become easier. In fact on newer boats, where skippers have to catch more fish, to pay their way, it becomes harder for the crews because they have more fish to handle.

PETERHEAD FISHING SKIPPER, 1979

Well, I don't know – you see, in a town like this, 'n that, in those days, there only seemed to be two jobs for the lads. They either wanted to go to sea or down the pit. And the majority of them wanted to go to sea, the sea seemed to be in a lad's blood, not like now, you never hear ships mentioned among young people now, it's not a seafarin' town, not like it was then. You couldn't throw a brick in the air but what it would come down on a seafarin' man's house, in Shields then, in those days.

HERBERT BRIGHT, *Ship's Cook (Retired)*, 1971

I mean to say, there was nothing else here, we never looked forward to anything else but the sea. There was no other employment.

MAGNUS MALCOLMSON, *AB (Retired)*, 1972

All I can remember is that ever since I was a very small child I always wanted to be a sailor . . . and then people told me, 'Oh, girls can't be sailors' and I forgot about it for a few years until I heard that a girl had been accepted as a cadet, and I thought, 'Well, blow this – if she can do it, I'm damn sure I can' and by pure stubbornness I persuaded them to take me on, and I like what I know about the job now, it's really interesting, never boring, because it's always so different, the stuff you're carrying and what you've got to do with it, and there's just lots and lots to learn. And I think . . . I don't know if I'm the only person that feels that, but even at sea I think it's interesting because I can spend hours just gazing at stars and sea and waves going by, and phosphorescence, and whales and seals and seagulls – on long passages where there isn't anything to look at, and no ships and no shore line and no lights of any kind, I can spend all night gazing at stars and meteors and things like that and it doesn't get boring at all.

NINA BAKER, *Second Mate*, 1979

I'll tell you now, its a freedom I've got. I've never been a person that can be cooped up in any inside job. I've got to be somewhere where it's outdoors, out and away. Somewhere where it's free, put it that way. I could never work in a factory where you were confined. That's why I've stayed at sea all these years.

JAMES PACK, *Bo'sun*, 1979

The astonishing, amazing sea has been there since time began – the great cleanser, the purifier, the climate-maker, weather-breeder, source of water and of life.

ALAN VILLIERS, 1963

Hutchinson and Co (Publishers) Ltd
An Imprint of the Hutchinson Publishing Group
3 Fitzroy Square, London W1P 6JD

Hutchinson Group (Australia) Pty Ltd
30–32 Cremorne Street, Richmond South, Victoria 3121
PO Box 151, Broadway, New South Wales 2007

Hutchinson Group (NZ) Ltd
32–34 View Road, PO Box 40-086, Glenfield, Auckland 10

Hutchinson Group (SA) (Pty) Ltd
PO Box 237, Bergvlei 2012, South Africa

ISBN 0 09 141951 4 (paper)
      0 09 141950 6 (hard cover)

In association with
The British Broadcasting Corporation
35 Marylebone High Street, London W1M 4AA

ISBN 0563 17852 3

and The National Maritime Museum, Greenwich.

First published 1980
© Michael Mason, Basil Greenhill and Robin Craig 1980

Printed and bound in Great Britain by Balding & Mansell,
Wisbech, Cambridgeshire.

Acknowledgments are due to the copyright holders for permission to reprint extracts from: Rachel Carson, *The Sea Around Us* (MacGibbon & Kee, 1964), Alan Villiers, *Oceans of the World* (Museum Press, 1963), Walter Runciman, *Collier Brigs and their Sailors* (Conway Maritime Press, 1972), Rudyard Kipling, 'M'Andrew's Hymn' (Macmillan), Ripyard Cuddling (Jack Davitt) *Shipyard Muddling* (Erdesdun Publications), Clare Francis, *Come Hell or High Water* (Pelham Books, 1977), T. S. Eliot, 'The Dry Salvages' (Faber, 1943). Also to the National Maritime Museum Oral History Collection, the BBC Sound Archives, the Trevor Lummis Collection, the BBC Archives, and 'Yesterday's Witness', BBC TV.

Photographic credits

Prelims and Chapter 1 Ben Backstay (Pollocks Toy Museum), photo by F. M. Sutcliffe (Sutcliffe Gallery), *The Return of the Runaway* by Joseph Clark (Laing Art Gallery/Tyne and Wear Museums), Queen's and Coburg Docks, 1895 (Liverpool Public Libraries) Harrison Chronometer (NMM), Mappamundi c.1791 (Beaurain), Earth from Space (NASA), Bahama sand shoal (NASA), Marine organism (Heather Angel), Divers with shark (Bacardi Rum UK), HMS *Aurora* (T. Brennan, HMS Drake), Whitby fisherman, F. M. Sutcliffe (Sutcliffe Gallery), *Golden Hinde* replica (Neil Jinkerson/Colour Processing Laboratories), (NMM), Rigging of *Mayflower II* (Beken of Cowes), (NMM), Bow of *Otago* (De Maus Collection, Turnbull Library, Wellington), Certificates (NMM), Crew of *Evelyn* (Gwynedd Archives), Sheet music (Mander & Mitchenson), Attack on Convoy, 1940 (IWM), Poster and Gillray caricature, (NMM), Coasting Pylot (NMM), Divers (Shell), Whitby fishermen (Sutcliffe Gallery).

Chapter 2 Sailing ship (Basil Greenhill, NMM), Fishermen, photo by D. O. Hill 1845 (National Portrait Gallery), Documents (NMM), Seaman splicing wire (Popperfoto), Taking in sail (NMM), Manning pumps: photo by Herbert Ponting (Popperfoto), Decks awash (Popperfoto), Hauling on braces (NMM), *Golden Hinde* (Beken of Cowes), Helmsman, and mate of *Cutty Sark* (NMM), Work on deck, capstan; log entries; fo'c's'le; and portrait of Bosun Bradshaw (all NMM), Gundeck of *Victory* (C.O. HMS *Victory*), Lower Deck (courtesy John Winton), Barque *King Malcolm* (Popperfoto), Captain Moody, *Cutty Sark* (NMM).

Chapter 3 A Sea Grammar (NMM), Ship in full sail (Popperfoto), Oak Forest (Forestry Commission), Elizabethan ship (NMM), Clinchbuilt hull at Marstal (Basil Greenhill), James Goss (NMM), Caulker's Mallet (NMM), Shipyard of A. Hall & Co, 1862 (NMM), Ship Model (NMM), Plan of *Express* (NMM), *Coastal Guide*, 1612 (Edinburgh U.L.), Sextant and Sounding Lead (NMM), Skipper Glanville (Town Dock Museum, Kingston upon Hull), Underwater photo (Peter Scoones/Seaphot).

Chapter 4 Whitby upper harbour, by F. M. Sutcliffe (Sutcliffe Gallery), Swansea

Docks in 1840's (NMM), Bill of lading (NMM), *Elizabeth* (R. Craig), Broker and shareholders' agreement, (Lloyds of London), Panorama of Thames 1749 (GLC), Phineas Pett (NPG), Newmarch Lee (NMM), *Aurora* figurehead (T. Brennan, HMS *Drake*), Rowlandson print (NMM), Seaman's wife (NMM), Man on steps (Liverpool Public Libraries), Recruiting poster, surgeon's instruments (NMM), Grinling Gibbons' fireplace in Admiralty Boardroom (DOE), Sea photo (Inst. of Oceanographic Sciences).

Chapter 5 Drake's cup (Plymouth City Museum), Drake's eyes from engraving by Van de Passe (NMM), Hilliard miniature of Drake (NPG), Coastal chart (NMM), Plancius 'Orbis Terrarum Typus', 1592 (British Library), Whitby fisherman (Sutcliffe Gallery), Whole Earth (NASA), James Cook by John Webber (National Art Gallery, Wellington), *Endeavour* (NMM), *Aurora* figurehead (T. Brennan), Tahitian girl (UTA French Airlines), *Terra Nova* off Cape Evans, Captain Scott (both Popperfoto), Deep Quest Submarine (Lockheed).

Chapter 6 Sail and Steam (R. Craig), Fo'c's'le, Rigging Passat (courtesy Anne Stanley), Captain's cabin, *Lynton*, Merchant sailing vessel (all NMM), Officer on SS *Lucania* (NMM), Captain Smith of SS *Athens* (NMM), Stoker (Dennis Stonham), Tramp (R. Craig), Captain Lincoln Colcord, Master of State of Maine (Penobscot Marine Museum via Basil Greenhill), Sea (3 photos NMM), HMS *Terrible* showing ram (Keeper of Scottish records), Taking in sail (NMM), Captain Sir Nowell Salmon, RN, VC (NMM), Scrubbing and Coaling (NMM), Fishermen (NMM), Memorial tiles, All Saints, Brightlingsea (Stephen Wakeling), Fishing photos (Syndication International).

Chapter 7 HMS *Resolution* firing salvo (IWM), 3rd Rates in Channel Squadron, 1840's (E. J. Martin), HMS *Cambridge* firing, by G. W. Wilson (Kodak), Elizabeth ship model (NMM), *Queen Mary* at Jutland (IWM), Glorious First of June, de Louthebourg (NMM), *Victory* gunports (C.O., HMS Victory), SS *Kemmendine* sinking, 1941 (4 photos: Popperfoto), Survivor – hysterical Lascar seaman (Popperfoto), Wreck off Libya (Peter Scoones/Seaphot), Lord Collingwood, by H. Howard (NPG), HMS *Barham* (WM), Tanker fire (Popperfoto), Figurehead HMS *Daring* (NMM).

Chapter 8 Screws of *Aquitania* (NMM), Brunel at Millwall (NMM),

Great Eastern at Millwall (NMM), HMS *Ramilles* launched (Keeper of Scottish Records), Certificate of Ass. Shipwrights Soc. (Sunderland Museum & Art Gallery), Hull of *Aquitania* (NMM), Paddle engines, P.S. *Lord of Isles*, 1891 (Science Museum), John Penn's marine works (NMM), Luncheon Menu, *Titanic* (Lloyds of London), 1st Class passengers on *Queen Mary* (Stewart Bale Ltd), Union Line Gazette list (R. Craig), 2nd Class Cabin, *Saxonia* (NMM), Engines of *City of New York*, Clydebank (Keeper of Scottish Records), Queen Elizabeth 1 at John Brown's (Stewart Bale Ltd).

Chapter 9 Dock scene (Science Museum), Sir Thomas Sutherland (P & O), *City of Paris* under construction (Keeper of Scottish Records), Prince's Dock, Hull by Atkinson Grimshaw (Ferens Gallery, Kingston upon Hull), Sailors at Liverpool (BBC Hulton), W. H. G. Kingston (Mersey Mission to Seamen), Charge sheet (Merseyside County Museum), HMS *Aurora* figurehead (T. Brennan, HMS *Drake*), Vegetable sellers 1890 (Liverpool Public Library), 'Exporting Cattle not for Insurance' (NMM), Public House (Liverpool City Council), Barmaid (BBC Hulton), Canterbury Music Hall, Lambeth (BBC Hulton), Advance note (Merseyside County Museum), Appledore Quay (NMM).

Chapter 10 Waves (Popperfoto), Goodwin Lightship wreck, 1954 (Popperfoto), Shipwreck victims (F. E. Gibson), Samuel Plimsoll (NMM), Ballad (Manchester Public Libraries), Wreck (NMM), Timbers on beach, the *Khyber* 1905 and wreck, the *Minnehaha*, 1874 (both F. E. Gibson), Trawler in gale (John Dyson), *Titanic* lifeboat (Walter Lord Collection), Iceberg (Mickleburg/Ardea), Lifeboat by Pamir (Royal National Lifeboat Institution), Crosswell Lifeboat (Syndication International).

Chapter 11 Earth Photo (NASA), Sextant and Chronometer (NMM), Computerized engineroom controls (Esso), Collision Avoidance System (Sperry Marine Systems), Oil carrier (Esso), Volunteer on beach, Portsall, (Popperfoto), Oil rig (Shell) submersible drilling platform (Shell), *Torrey Canyon* (Popperfoto), Tanker sinking (Royal National Mission to Deepsea Fishermen), Grain Silos (P.L.A., Handford), Polaris missile (C.O.I.), Coaster in seas (Skyfotos), Humpback whale off Newfoundland (Friends of the Earth).